THE ZANZIBAR ADVENTURE: A TRAVEL PREPARATION GUIDE

SHONDA WILLIAMS

All images in this book are from pexels.com

Table of Contents

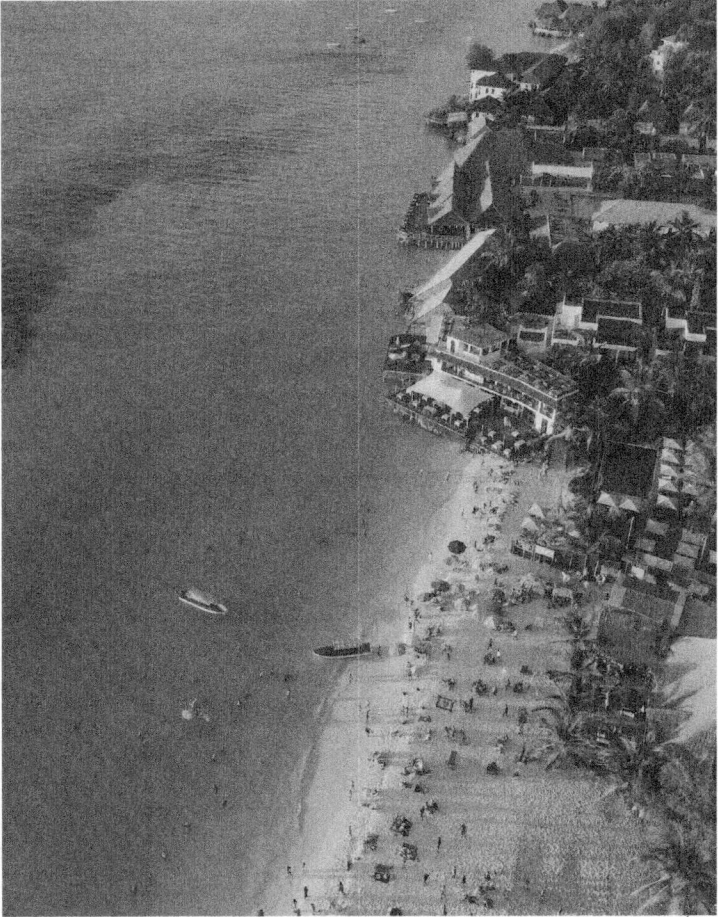

Introduction

Located off the coast of Tanzania, Zanzibar is a semi-autonomous island that is steeped in history, culture, and natural beauty. This enchanting archipelago is a melting pot of African, Arab, and European influences, making it a unique and fascinating destination for travelers.

From the snow-white beaches and crystal-clear waters of the Indian Ocean to the ancient stone town of Zanzibar City, with its narrow alleys, bustling markets, and historic landmarks, there is no shortage of exciting things to see and do in Zanzibar.

Whether you're a history buff, a beach lover, a foodie, or an adventure-seeker, Zanzibar has something for everyone. In this travel guide, we'll take you on a journey through the best of Zanzibar, from its stunning natural beauty and rich cultural heritage to its delicious cuisine and exciting activities.

So, get ready to immerse yourself in the magic of Zanzibar, and discover why this incredible island is fast becoming one of Africa's most popular tourist destinations.

In the following pages, we'll take you on a tour of Zanzibar, covering everything from the best places to stay, eat, and drink to the top attractions, activities, and experiences.

We'll also provide you with insider tips and advice on how to make the most of your trip to Zanzibar, from navigating the local transportation system to avoiding the crowds and finding the best deals.

Whether you're a seasoned traveler or just starting to plan your trip, this guide is designed to be your ultimate resource for all things Zanzibar.

So, let's get started and discover the magic of Zanzibar together!

Chapter 1 • Welcome to Zanzibar

Brief History of Zanzibar

Located off the coast of Tanzania, Zanzibar has a rich and fascinating history that spans over 1,000 years. From its early days as a trading post to its current status as a semi-autonomous island, Zanzibar has been shaped by a diverse array of cultures, empires, and influences.

Ancient Trading Post (1000 AD - 1500 AD)

Zanzibar's history began in the 10th century, when it was established as a trading post by Arab merchants. The island's strategic location on the Indian Ocean trade route made it an ideal hub for the exchange of goods such as spices, textiles, and precious metals.

Portuguese Colonization (1500 AD - 1698 AD)

In the early 16th century, Zanzibar was colonized by the Portuguese, who established a fortified trading post on the island. The Portuguese brought with them their language, culture, and architecture, which had a lasting impact on the island.

Omani Rule (1698 AD - 1890 AD)

In 1698, Zanzibar was captured by the Omanis, who ruled the island for nearly two centuries. During this period, Zanzibar became a major center for the slave trade, with thousands of Africans being transported to the island and beyond.

British Protectorate (1890 AD - 1963 AD)

In 1890, Zanzibar became a British protectorate, with the British exercising control over the island's foreign affairs. During this period, Zanzibar underwent significant modernization, with the establishment of a new constitution, a modern education system, and improved infrastructure.

Independence and Union with Tanzania (1963 AD - present)

On December 19, 1963, Zanzibar gained its independence from Britain and became a sovereign state. However, just a month later, Zanzibar merged with Tanganyika to form the United Republic of Tanzania, with Zanzibar becoming a semi-autonomous region within the new country.

Today, Zanzibar is a thriving island with a rich cultural heritage and a strong sense of identity. Its history is a testament to the power of cultural exchange and the resilience of its people.

Why Visit Zanzibar?

Stunning Beaches: Zanzibar is home to some of the most beautiful beaches in the world, with pristine white sand and crystal-clear waters that are perfect for swimming, snorkeling, and diving.

Rich History and Culture: Zanzibar has a rich and fascinating history, with a unique blend of African, Arab, and European influences. Visit the ancient stone town of Zanzibar City, with its narrow alleys, bustling markets, and historic landmarks.

Delicious Cuisine: Zanzibari cuisine is a delicious blend of African, Arab, and Indian flavors, with popular dishes like urojo (a spicy soup), nyama choma (roasted meat), and mandazi (fried doughnuts).

Vibrant Nightlife: Zanzibar has a lively nightlife scene, with everything from beach bars and clubs to live music venues and traditional dance performances.

Water Sports and Activities: Zanzibar is a paradise for water sports enthusiasts, with opportunities for snorkeling, diving, kayaking, paddleboarding, and more.

Fascinating Wildlife: Zanzibar is home to a wide range of wildlife, including dolphins, whales, and sea turtles. Take a boat tour or visit the Zanzibar Butterfly Centre to see these amazing creatures up close.

Relaxation and Wellness: Zanzibar is the perfect destination for relaxation and wellness, with numerous spas, yoga studios, and wellness centers offering a range of treatments and activities.

Unique Shopping Experiences: Zanzibar is a shopper's paradise, with numerous markets, bazaars, and boutiques selling everything from traditional handicrafts to modern fashion and jewelry.

Festivals and Events: Zanzibar hosts a range of festivals and events throughout the year, including the Zanzibar International Film Festival, the Zanzibar Music Festival, and the Eid al-Fitr celebrations.

Affordability: Zanzibar is an affordable destination, with a range of accommodation options, from budget-friendly guesthouses to luxury resorts, and a wide range of activities and attractions to suit all budgets.

Chapter 2 • Planning Your Trip

Best Time to Visit Zanzibar

In this guide, we'll take you through the best times to visit Zanzibar, including the weather, festivals, and events.

Zanzibar's Climate

Zanzibar has a tropical climate, with two main seasons: the dry season and the wet season. The dry season runs from June to October, and is characterized by warm and sunny weather, with average temperatures ranging from 25-30°C (77-86°F). The wet season runs from November to May, and is characterized by hot and humid weather, with frequent rain showers and average temperatures ranging from 28-32°C (82-90°F).

Best Time to Visit Zanzibar

Based on the climate, the best time to visit Zanzibar is during the dry season, from June to October. During this time, the weather is warm and sunny, making it ideal for swimming, snorkeling, and diving. Additionally, the dry season is the best time to visit Zanzibar's famous beaches, such as Nungwi Beach and Kendwa Beach.

Festivals and Events

Zanzibar is known for its vibrant culture, and there are many festivals and events that take place throughout the year. Some of the top festivals and events in Zanzibar include:

- Zanzibar International Film Festival: Held every year in July, this festival showcases the best of African and international cinema.

- Zanzibar Music Festival: Held every year in February, this festival features a lineup of local and international musicians.

- Eid al-Fitr: Celebrated by Muslims around the world, Eid al-Fitr is a major festival in Zanzibar, and is marked by feasting, gift-giving, and other celebrations.

- Zanzibar Beach Festival: Held every year in August, this festival features a range of activities, including swimming, snorkeling, and diving, as well as live music and dancing.

Avoiding the Crowds

If you're looking to avoid the crowds, the best time to visit Zanzibar is during the shoulder season, from April to May or September to November. During this time, the weather is still warm and sunny, but the crowds are smaller, making it easier to explore the island and enjoy its many attractions.

Zanzibar is a year-round destination, but the best time to visit depends on your preferences. If you're looking for warm and sunny weather, the dry season from June to October is the best time to visit. If you're looking to avoid the crowds, the shoulder season from April to May or September to November is the best time to visit. Whatever time of year you visit, Zanzibar is sure to captivate you with its stunning beaches, vibrant culture, and warm hospitality.

Getting to and around Zanzibar

Getting to Zanzibar

By Air

The fastest way to get to Zanzibar is by flying into Abeid Amane Karume International Airport (ZNZ), which is located about 5 kilometers south of Stone Town. The airport receives flights from major airlines such as Ethiopian Airlines, Kenya Airways, and Turkish Airlines, as well as regional airlines like Precision Air and ZanAir.

By Ferry

Another way to get to Zanzibar is by ferry from Dar es Salaam, Tanzania's largest city. The ferry ride takes about 2 hours and offers stunning views of the Indian Ocean. There are several ferry operators, including Azam Marine and Sea Express, that offer daily departures from Dar es Salaam.

By Dhow

For a more traditional and adventurous way to get to Zanzibar, consider taking a dhow (a traditional sailing boat) from Dar es Salaam or other nearby islands. The journey takes about 4-6 hours, depending on the wind and sea conditions.

Getting Around Zanzibar

By Taxi

Taxis are widely available in Zanzibar and are a convenient way to get around the island. You can hire a taxi for a day or negotiate a fare for a specific journey. Make sure to agree on the fare before you start your journey.

By Rental Car

Renting a car is a great way to explore Zanzibar at your own pace. There are several car rental companies on the island, including Europcar and Avis, that offer a range of vehicles from economy cars to SUVs.

By Bicycle

Zanzibar is a relatively flat island, making it easy to explore by bicycle. You can rent bicycles in Stone Town or other major towns on the island.

By Dala-Dala

Dala-dalas are local buses that operate on fixed routes around the island. They are a cheap and fun way to get around, but can be crowded and unpredictable.

On Foot

Finally, Zanzibar is a great island to explore on foot. Stone Town, in particular, is a fascinating place to wander around, with its narrow alleys, bustling markets, and historic landmarks.

Currency and Money Matters

The Tanzanian Shilling: The Official Currency of Tanzania

The Tanzanian shilling (TZS) is the official currency of Tanzania, and it's also widely accepted in Zanzibar. The shilling is divided into 100 senti, and it's available in denominations of 500, 1,000, 2,000, 5,000, and 10,000 shillings.

Exchanging Currency in Zanzibar

You can exchange your currency for Tanzanian shillings at a bank, currency exchange office, or a hotel. The exchange rates may vary depending on the location and the time of day. It's always a good idea to have some local currency with you when you arrive in Zanzibar, especially if you plan to take a taxi or bus from the airport.

Using ATMs in Zanzibar

ATMs are widely available in Zanzibar, especially in Stone Town and other major tourist areas. You can withdraw Tanzanian shillings using your debit or credit card. Be aware that you may be charged a withdrawal fee by your bank, as well as a conversion fee.

Credit Cards and Mobile Payments in Zanzibar

Credit cards are widely accepted in Zanzibar, especially in tourist areas and high-end hotels. Mobile payments like M-Pesa and Tigo Pesa are also popular in Zanzibar, especially among locals. However, it's always a good idea to have some cash with you, especially when visiting local markets or taking a taxi.

Tips and Essentials for Managing Your Money in Zanzibar

- Always have some local currency with you, especially when arriving in Zanzibar.
- Use reputable currency exchange offices or banks to exchange your currency.
- Be aware of the exchange rates and any fees associated with exchanging currency.
- Use ATMs to withdraw local currency, but be aware of any withdrawal fees.
- Have a backup credit or debit card in case your primary card is lost or stolen.
- Always keep your valuables secure and be mindful of your surroundings, especially in crowded areas.

Budgeting and Costs in Zanzibar

Zanzibar can be a relatively affordable destination, especially if you're willing to stay in budget-friendly accommodations and eat at local restaurants. Below are some approximate costs to help you budget for your trip:

Accommodation: $10-50 per night for a budget-friendly hotel or guesthouse

Food: $5-15 per meal for a local restaurant or street food

Transportation: $5-10 per ride for a taxi or $1-2 per ride for a dala-dala (local bus)

Activities: $20-50 per person for a snorkeling or diving trip, $10-20 per person for a guided tour of Stone Town

Chapter 3 • Zanzibari Culture and Etiquette

Zanzibari Languages and Basic Phrases

Languages Spoken in Zanzibar

Zanzibar is a multilingual society, with several languages spoken on the island. The main languages spoken in Zanzibar are:

Swahili: Also known as Kiswahili, Swahili is the official language of Tanzania and is widely spoken in Zanzibar. It's a Bantu language that is closely related to other languages spoken in East Africa.

English: English is widely spoken in Zanzibar, particularly in tourist areas and among businesspeople. Many Zanzibaris speak English as a second language, and it's often used as a lingua franca.

Arabic: Arabic is also spoken in Zanzibar, particularly among the island's Muslim population. Many Zanzibaris learn Arabic as a second language, and it's often used in Islamic schools and mosques.

Basic Phrases in Swahili

Learning a few basic phrases in Swahili can go a long way in making your trip to Zanzibar more enjoyable. Below are some basic phrases to get you started:

- Hello: Jambo (JAHM-boh)

- Goodbye: Kwaheri (KWAH-heh-ree)

- Thank you: Asante (AH-sahnt-eh)

- Yes: Ndiyo (n-DEE-yoh)

- No: Hapana (HAH-pah-nah)

- How much is this?: Ni bei gani hii? (NEE BAY GAH-nee HEE)

- Where is...?: Wapi...? (WAH-pee)

- I don't understand: Sijaelewa (SEE-jah-eh-LEH-wah)

Basic Phrases in Arabic

If you're visiting Zanzibar during Ramadan or other Islamic holidays, learning a few basic phrases in Arabic can be a nice gesture. Below are some basic phrases to get you started:

- Hello: As-salamu alaykum (AH-sah-LAH-moo AH-lee-KOOM)

- Goodbye: Wa alaykum as-salam (WAH AH-lee-KOOM AH-sah-LAH-moo)

- Thank you: Shukraan (SHOO-krah-n)

- Yes: Na'am (NAH-am)

- No: Laa (LAH-ah)

Tips for Communicating with Locals

- Learn a few basic phrases: Learning a few basic phrases in Swahili or Arabic can go a long way in making your trip more enjoyable.

- Use hand gestures: Hand gestures can be a useful way to communicate when you don't speak the local language.

- Ask for help: Don't be afraid to ask for help when you need it. Many Zanzibaris are happy to assist tourists and practice their English language skills.

- Be patient and respectful: Communication can be challenging when you don't speak the local language. Be patient and respectful, and don't get frustrated if you don't understand something at first.

Cultural Norms and Customs

In this guide, we'll cover the cultural norms and customs you should be aware of when visiting Zanzibar.

Ramadan and Islamic Holidays

Zanzibar is a predominantly Muslim island, and Ramadan and other Islamic holidays are observed with great enthusiasm. Below are some tips for respecting local customs during Ramadan and other Islamic holidays:

- Avoid eating and drinking in public: During Ramadan, Muslims fast from dawn to sunset, and it's considered impolite to eat and drink in public.
- Be respectful of mosque hours: Mosques are closed to visitors during prayer times, so be sure to check the prayer schedule before visiting.
- Avoid loud music and noise: During Ramadan and other Islamic holidays, loud music and noise are considered impolite.

Interacting with Locals

Zanzibaris are known for their warm hospitality, and interacting with locals can be a rewarding and enriching experience. Below are some tips for interacting with locals:

- Use formal titles: When interacting with older Zanzibaris, use formal titles such as "Mzee" (respected elder) or "Bibi" (respected lady).
- Show respect for elders: In Zanzibari culture, elders are highly respected, so be sure to show deference to older locals.

- Avoid public displays of affection: Public displays of affection, such as kissing or hugging, are considered impolite in Zanzibari culture.

Gift-Giving

Gift-giving is an important part of Zanzibari culture, and it's considered impolite to arrive at someone's home empty-handed. Below are some tips for gift-giving in Zanzibar:

- Bring a small gift: When visiting a local home, bring a small gift, such as a basket of fruit or a box of sweets.

- Avoid expensive gifts: Avoid giving expensive gifts, as this can be seen as impolite or even insulting.

- Gifts for children: If you're visiting a local home with children, consider bringing a small gift, such as a toy or a book.

Zanzibar is a culturally rich and diverse island, and respecting local customs and traditions is essential for a positive and enriching experience. By following the tips and guidelines outlined in this guide, you can ensure a respectful and enjoyable trip to Zanzibar. Remember to be open-minded, curious, and respectful, and you'll be sure to have a fantastic time in this incredible island paradise.

Dining Etiquette

Dining in Zanzibar is a culinary adventure that offers a unique blend of African, Arab, and European flavors. However, when dining in Zanzibar, it's essential to respect local customs and traditions to ensure a positive and enjoyable experience. In this guide, we'll cover the dining etiquette you should know when visiting Zanzibar.

Table Manners

When dining in Zanzibar, table manners are important to show respect for your host and the local culture. Below are some tips to keep in mind:

Use your right hand: In Zanzibari culture, the left hand is considered unclean, so it's best to use your right hand when eating.

Wait for the host to start eating: When dining with locals, wait for the host to start eating before you begin.

Eat with your hands: In many Zanzibari restaurants, eating with your hands is the norm. Make sure to wash your hands before eating.

Don't leave the table until everyone is finished: In Zanzibari culture, it's considered impolite to leave the table until everyone is finished eating.

Restaurant Etiquette

When dining in restaurants in Zanzibar, below are some etiquette tips to keep in mind:

Dress modestly: When dining in restaurants, dress modestly and avoid revealing clothing.

Remove your shoes: In some Zanzibari restaurants, it's customary to remove your shoes before entering.

Use a napkin: Use a napkin to wipe your hands and mouth before and after eating.

Tip your server: Tipping your server is not mandatory, but it's appreciated for good service.

Street Food Etiquette

When eating street food in Zanzibar, below are some etiquette tips to keep in mind:

Eat at a reputable stall: Make sure to eat at a reputable stall that is popular with locals.

Use a utensil or your right hand: Use a utensil or your right hand to eat street food.

Don't eat in public during Ramadan: During Ramadan, it's considered impolite to eat in public, so make sure to eat in a private area.

Pay the correct price: Make sure to pay the correct price for your street food, and don't try to haggle.

Special Dietary Requirements

When dining in Zanzibar, it's essential to be mindful of special dietary requirements. Below are some tips to keep in mind:

Halal food: Zanzibar is a predominantly Muslim island, and most restaurants serve halal food. However, it's always a good idea to check with your server to confirm.

Vegetarian and vegan options: Many Zanzibari restaurants offer vegetarian and vegan options, but it's always a good idea to check with your server to confirm.

- Food allergies: If you have a food allergy, make sure to inform your server before ordering.

Dress Code and Fashion

Zanzibar is a tropical island with a rich cultural heritage, and dressing respectfully is essential to having a positive and enjoyable experience. In this guide, we'll cover the dress code and fashion tips you need to know when traveling to Zanzibar.

Dress Code Essentials

When it comes to dressing in Zanzibar, there are a few essentials to keep in mind:

- Dress modestly: Zanzibar is a conservative island, and you should dress modestly to respect local customs. Avoid revealing clothing, such as short shorts, tank tops, or low-cut dresses.

- Cover your shoulders and knees: When visiting mosques, temples, or other cultural sites, make sure to cover your shoulders and knees as a sign of respect.

- Wear lightweight and breathable clothing: Zanzibar is a tropical island, and the heat and humidity can be intense. Wear lightweight and breathable clothing, such as cotton or linen, to stay cool and comfortable.

- Bring a scarf or shawl: A scarf or shawl can be a useful accessory in Zanzibar, as it can help protect you from the sun, wind, and dust.

Fashion Tips

When it comes to fashion in Zanzibar, there are a few tips to keep in mind:

- Dress for the occasion: Zanzibar is a formal island, and you should dress accordingly for different occasions. For example, if you're visiting a mosque or attending a formal event, dress in more formal attire.

- Add a touch of local flair: Zanzibar is known for its vibrant textiles and colorful clothing. Add a touch of local flair to your outfit with a traditional Zanzibari scarf, shawl, or piece of clothing.

- Don't forget sunscreen and a hat: Zanzibar is a tropical island, and the sun can be intense. Don't forget to pack sunscreen and a hat to protect yourself from the sun.

- Wear comfortable shoes: Zanzibar is a walking island, and you'll likely do a lot of walking during your trip. Wear comfortable shoes that are suitable for walking.

Beach and Waterwear

When it comes to beach and waterwear in Zanzibar, there are a few things to keep in mind:

- Swimwear should be modest: While swimwear is acceptable on the beach, it's still important to dress modestly. Avoid revealing swimwear, such as bikinis or speedos.

- Cover up when leaving the beach: When leaving the beach, cover up with a lightweight dress, shirt, or pants to respect local customs.

- Wear a rash guard or wetsuit: Zanzibar is known for its strong currents and coral reefs, so it's a good idea to wear a rash guard or wetsuit when swimming or snorkeling.

Nighttime Attire

When it comes to nighttime attire in Zanzibar, there are a few things to keep in mind:

- Dress up for dinner: Zanzibar is a formal island, and you should dress up for dinner at a restaurant or hotel.

- Avoid revealing clothing: Avoid revealing clothing, such as short shorts or low-cut dresses, when going out at night.

- Add a touch of elegance: Add a touch of elegance to your outfit with a scarf, shawl, or piece of jewelry.

Festivals and Celebrations

Zanzibar is a vibrant island with a rich cultural heritage, and festivals and celebrations are an integral part of island life. Throughout the year, Zanzibar hosts a range of exciting events that showcase the island's unique blend of African, Arab, and European influences.

January: Zanzibar International Film Festival

The Zanzibar International Film Festival (ZIFF) is one of the largest film festivals in East Africa, showcasing a range of local and international films. The festival takes place in January and features a range of events, including film screenings, workshops, and live music performances.

February: Sauti za Busara Music Festival

The Sauti za Busara Music Festival is a popular music festival that takes place in February. The festival features a range of local and international musicians, performing a variety of genres, including traditional Tanzanian music, Afrobeat, and reggae.

March: Zanzibar Beach Festival

The Zanzibar Beach Festival is a fun and lively event that takes place in March. The festival features a range of activities, including beach volleyball, soccer, and swimming competitions, as well as live music performances and traditional dances.

April: Easter Celebrations

Easter is an important holiday in Zanzibar, and the island's Christian community comes together to celebrate with traditional church services, processions, and feasts.

May: Eid al-Fitr Celebrations

Eid al-Fitr is a significant holiday in the Islamic calendar, marking the end of Ramadan. In Zanzibar, Eid al-Fitr is celebrated with traditional prayers, feasts, and gift-giving.

June: Zanzibar International Triathlon

The Zanzibar International Triathlon is a popular sporting event that takes place in June. The event features a range of triathlon distances, including sprint, Olympic, and half-Ironman distances.

July: Zanzibar Cultural Festival

The Zanzibar Cultural Festival is a celebration of the island's rich cultural heritage. The festival features a range of traditional dances, music performances, and cultural exhibitions.

August: Zanzibar Beach Soccer Tournament

The Zanzibar Beach Soccer Tournament is a fun and exciting event that takes place in August. The tournament features a range of local and international teams competing in beach soccer matches.

September: Eid al-Hajj Celebrations

Eid al-Hajj is a significant holiday in the Islamic calendar, marking the end of the Hajj pilgrimage. In Zanzibar, Eid al-Hajj is celebrated with traditional prayers, feasts, and gift-giving.

October: Zanzibar International Marathon

The Zanzibar International Marathon is a popular sporting event that takes place in October. The event features a range of marathon distances, including full marathon, half marathon, and 10km distances.

November: Zanzibar Music and Arts Festival

The Zanzibar Music and Arts Festival is a celebration of the island's vibrant music and arts scene. The festival features a range of live music performances, art exhibitions, and cultural workshops.

December: Christmas and New Year's Celebrations

Christmas and New Year's are popular holidays in Zanzibar, and the island's Christian community comes together to celebrate with traditional church services, processions, and feasts.

Chapter 4 • Exploring Zanzibar

Stone Town

Stone Town is the oldest part of Zanzibar City, and it's a place where ancient traditions and modern culture blend seamlessly together. This historic town is a UNESCO World Heritage Site, and it's a must-visit destination for anyone traveling to Zanzibar.

Top Attractions in Stone Town

Stone Town is a treasure trove of historical landmarks, cultural attractions, and traditional markets. Below are some of the top attractions to visit in Stone Town:

House of Wonders: This historic building is one of the most iconic landmarks in Stone Town. It was built in 1883 and features a unique blend of Arabic, European, and African architectural styles.

Old Fort: The Old Fort is a 17th-century fort that was built by the Portuguese. Today, it's a popular cultural center that hosts traditional music and dance performances.

Slave Market Museum: The Slave Market Museum is a poignant reminder of Zanzibar's dark past as a major slave trading hub. The museum features a collection of artifacts and exhibits that tell the story of the transatlantic slave trade.

Darajani Market: The Darajani Market is a bustling marketplace that sells everything from fresh produce to traditional handicrafts. It's a great place to experience the sights, sounds, and smells of Stone Town.

Forodhani Night Food Market: The Forodhani Night Food Market is a popular night market that takes place every evening in Stone Town. It's a great place to try traditional Zanzibari cuisine, including seafood, meat dishes, and vegetarian options.

Recommended Accommodation in Stone Town

236 Hurumzi: This boutique hotel is located in the heart of Stone Town and offers luxurious rooms and suites with traditional Zanzibari decor.

DoubleTree by Hilton Hotel Zanzibar - Stone Town: This modern hotel is located in the heart of Stone Town and offers comfortable rooms and suites with modern amenities.

Zanzibar Coffee House Hotel: This boutique hotel is located in a historic building in Stone Town and offers cozy rooms and suites with traditional Zanzibari decor.

Recommended Restaurants in Stone Town

The Tea House Restaurant: This restaurant is located in the heart of Stone Town and serves a wide range of traditional Zanzibari dishes, including seafood, meat dishes, and vegetarian options.

Forodhani Night Food Market: This night market is a great place to try traditional Zanzibari cuisine, including seafood, meat dishes, and vegetarian options.

Monsoon Restaurant: This restaurant is located in the heart of Stone Town and serves a wide range of international dishes, including Indian, Chinese, and Italian cuisine.

Nungwi

Nungwi is a charming fishing village located on the northern tip of Zanzibar. This picturesque village is known for its stunning beaches, crystal-clear waters, and vibrant marine life. Nungwi is a popular destination for travelers looking for a relaxing and peaceful getaway from the hustle and bustle of Stone Town.

Top Attractions in Nungwi

Nungwi Beach: Nungwi Beach is one of the most beautiful beaches in Zanzibar. The beach is lined with

palm trees, and the crystal-clear waters are perfect for swimming, snorkeling, and diving.

Mnarani Marine Park: The Mnarani Marine Park is a protected marine reserve that is home to a stunning array of marine life, including dolphins, whales, and sea turtles.

Nungwi Fish Market: The Nungwi Fish Market is a bustling marketplace where local fishermen sell their daily catch. The market is a great place to see the local seafood and learn about the fishing industry in Zanzibar.

Dhow Building Yard: The Dhow Building Yard is a traditional boat-building yard where local craftsmen build and repair traditional Zanzibari dhows.

Kendwa Beach: Kendwa Beach is a stunning beach located just north of Nungwi. The beach is known for its crystal-clear waters, powdery white sand, and vibrant coral reefs.

Recommended Accommodation in Nungwi

Ras Nungwi Beach Hotel: This luxury hotel is located on the beach in Nungwi and offers stunning views of the Indian Ocean. The hotel features comfortable rooms and suites, a swimming pool, and a range of activities, including snorkeling, diving, and fishing.

Nungwi Village Beach Resort: This resort is located in the heart of Nungwi and offers comfortable rooms and suites, a swimming pool, and a range of activities, including snorkeling, diving, and fishing.

Amaan Bungalows: This budget-friendly guesthouse is located in the heart of Nungwi and offers comfortable rooms and suites, a swimming pool, and a range of activities, including snorkeling, diving, and fishing.

Recommended Restaurants in Nungwi

The Fisherman's Restaurant: This restaurant is located on the beach in Nungwi and serves a wide range of fresh seafood dishes, including fish, lobster, and prawns.

The Beach House Restaurant: This restaurant is located in the heart of Nungwi and serves a wide range of international dishes, including Italian, Chinese, and Indian cuisine.

Mama's Restaurant: This restaurant is located in the heart of Nungwi and serves a wide range of traditional Zanzibari dishes, including ugali, sukuma wiki, and nyama choma.

Kendwa

Kendwa is a picturesque beach town located on the northwest coast of Zanzibar. This charming town is known for its stunning beaches, crystal-clear waters, and vibrant coral reefs. Kendwa is a popular destination for travelers looking for a relaxing and peaceful getaway from the hustle and bustle of Stone Town.

Top Attractions in Kendwa

Kendwa Beach: Kendwa Beach is one of the most beautiful beaches in Zanzibar. The beach is lined with palm trees, and the crystal-clear waters are perfect for swimming, snorkeling, and diving.

Kendwa Reef: The Kendwa Reef is a vibrant coral reef that is home to a stunning array of marine life, including fish, turtles, and dolphins.

Kendwa Sunset Cruise: The Kendwa Sunset Cruise is a popular activity that allows you to watch the sunset over the Indian Ocean while enjoying a relaxing cruise.

Kendwa Water Sports: Kendwa Water Sports is a popular water sports center that offers a range of activities, including snorkeling, diving, kayaking, and paddleboarding.

Kendwa Village Tour: The Kendwa Village Tour is a great way to experience the local culture and traditions of Kendwa. The tour takes you through the village, where you can see traditional homes, meet local residents, and learn about the history and customs of the area.

Recommended Accommodation in Kendwa

Kendwa Rocks Hotel: This luxury hotel is located on the beach in Kendwa and offers stunning views of the Indian Ocean. The hotel features comfortable rooms and suites, a swimming pool, and a range of activities, including snorkeling, diving, and fishing.

Kendwa Beach Resort: This resort is located on the beach in Kendwa and offers comfortable rooms and suites, a swimming pool, and a range of activities, including snorkeling, diving, and kayaking.

Sunset Kendwa Bungalows: This budget-friendly guesthouse is located in the heart of Kendwa and offers comfortable rooms and suites, a swimming pool, and a range of activities, including snorkeling, diving, and fishing.

Recommended Restaurants in Kendwa

The Beach House Restaurant: This restaurant is located on the beach in Kendwa and serves a wide range of international dishes, including seafood, meat dishes, and vegetarian options.

Kendwa Rocks Restaurant: This restaurant is located at the Kendwa Rocks Hotel and serves a wide range of traditional Zanzibari dishes, including seafood, meat dishes, and vegetarian options.

Sunset Kendwa Restaurant: This restaurant is located at the Sunset Kendwa Bungalows and serves a wide range of traditional Zanzibari dishes, including seafood, meat dishes, and vegetarian options.

Jambiani

Jambiani is a picturesque beach town located on the southeastern coast of Zanzibar. This secluded town is known for its stunning beaches, crystal-clear waters, and vibrant coral reefs. Jambiani is a popular destination for travelers looking for a relaxing and peaceful getaway from the hustle and bustle of Stone Town.

Top Attractions in Jambiani

Jambiani Beach: Jambiani Beach is one of the most beautiful beaches in Zanzibar. The beach is lined with palm trees, and the crystal-clear waters are perfect for swimming, snorkeling, and diving.

Paje Beach: Paje Beach is a stunning beach located just north of Jambiani. The beach is known for its crystal-clear waters, powdery white sand, and vibrant coral reefs.

Kizimkazi Dolphin Tour: The Kizimkazi Dolphin Tour is a popular activity that allows you to swim with dolphins in their natural habitat.

Jambiani Village Tour: The Jambiani Village Tour is a great way to experience the local culture and traditions of Jambiani. The tour takes you through the village, where you can see traditional homes, meet local residents, and learn about the history and customs of the area.

Jambiani Water Sports: Jambiani Water Sports is a popular water sports center that offers a range of activities, including snorkeling, diving, kayaking, and paddleboarding.

Recommended Accommodation in Jambiani

Blue Moon Resort: This luxury resort is located on the beach in Jambiani and offers stunning views of the Indian Ocean. The resort features comfortable rooms and suites, a swimming pool, and a range of activities, including snorkeling, diving, and fishing.

Jambiani Beach Resort: This resort is located on the beach in Jambiani and offers comfortable rooms and suites, a swimming pool, and a range of activities, including snorkeling, diving, and kayaking.

Coral Rock Hotel: This budget-friendly hotel is located in the heart of Jambiani and offers comfortable rooms and suites, a swimming pool, and a range of activities, including snorkeling, diving, and fishing.

Recommended Restaurants in Jambiani

The Beach House Restaurant: This restaurant is located on the beach in Jambiani and serves a wide range of international dishes, including seafood, meat dishes, and vegetarian options.

Jambiani Beach Restaurant: This restaurant is located on the beach in Jambiani and serves a wide range of traditional Zanzibari dishes, including seafood, meat dishes, and vegetarian options.

Coral Rock Restaurant: This restaurant is located at the Coral Rock Hotel and serves a wide range of international dishes, including seafood, meat dishes, and vegetarian options.

Paje

Paje is a picturesque beach town located on the southeastern coast of Zanzibar. This charming town is known for its stunning beaches, crystal-clear waters, and vibrant coral reefs. Paje is a popular destination for travelers looking for a relaxing and adventurous getaway from the hustle and bustle of Stone Town.

Top Attractions in Paje

Paje Beach: Paje Beach is one of the most beautiful beaches in Zanzibar. The beach is lined with palm trees, and the crystal-clear waters are perfect for swimming, snorkeling, and diving.

Kitesurfing and Windsurfing: Paje is known as the kitesurfing capital of Zanzibar, and it's a popular destination for kitesurfers and windsurfers. The town has several kitesurfing and windsurfing schools and rental shops.

Paje Dive Center: The Paje Dive Center is a popular dive center that offers scuba diving and snorkeling trips to the coral reefs and shipwrecks off the coast of Paje.

Paje Village Tour: The Paje Village Tour is a great way to experience the local culture and traditions of Paje. The tour takes you through the village, where you can see traditional homes, meet local residents, and learn about the history and customs of the area.

Jozani Forest National Park: The Jozani Forest National Park is a popular national park that is home to a wide range of flora and fauna, including the endangered red colobus monkey.

Recommended Accommodation in Paje

Paje Beach Resort: This resort is located on the beach in Paje and offers comfortable rooms and suites, a swimming pool, and a range of activities, including kitesurfing, windsurfing, and snorkeling.

Kite Centre Paje: This kitesurfing resort is located on the beach in Paje and offers comfortable rooms and suites, a swimming pool, and a range of kitesurfing and windsurfing activities.

Paje Guest House: This budget-friendly guesthouse is located in the heart of Paje and offers comfortable rooms and suites, a swimming pool, and a range of activities, including snorkeling, diving, and fishing.

Recommended Restaurants in Paje

The Beach House Restaurant: This restaurant is located on the beach in Paje and serves a wide range of international dishes, including seafood, meat dishes, and vegetarian options.

Paje Beach Restaurant: This restaurant is located on the beach in Paje and serves a wide range of traditional Zanzibari dishes, including seafood, meat dishes, and vegetarian options.

Kite Centre Paje Restaurant: This restaurant is located at the Kite Centre Paje and serves a wide range of international dishes, including seafood, meat dishes, and vegetarian options.

Matemwe

Matemwe is a picturesque fishing village located on the northeast coast of Zanzibar. This charming village is known for its stunning beaches, crystal-clear waters, and vibrant coral reefs. Matemwe is a popular destination for travelers looking for a relaxing and peaceful getaway from the hustle and bustle of Stone Town.

Top Attractions in Matemwe

Matemwe Beach: Matemwe Beach is one of the most beautiful beaches in Zanzibar. The beach is lined with palm trees, and the crystal-clear waters are perfect for swimming, snorkeling, and diving.

Mnemba Atoll: The Mnemba Atoll is a stunning coral reef that is located just off the coast of Matemwe. The atoll is home to a wide range of marine life, including fish, turtles, and dolphins.

Matemwe Village Tour: The Matemwe Village Tour is a great way to experience the local culture and traditions of Matemwe. The tour takes you through the village, where you can see traditional homes, meet local residents, and learn about the history and customs of the area.

Kiteboarding and Windsurfing: Matemwe is a popular destination for kiteboarders and windsurfers, with consistent winds and flat waters making it an ideal spot for these sports.

Fishing and Boat Trips: Matemwe is a fishing village, and there are plenty of opportunities to go fishing or take a boat trip to explore the surrounding waters.

Recommended Accommodation in Matemwe

Matemwe Beach House: This luxury beach house is located on the beach in Matemwe and offers stunning views of the Indian Ocean. The house features comfortable rooms and suites, a swimming pool, and a range of activities, including snorkeling, diving, and fishing.

Matemwe Retreat: This boutique hotel is located in the heart of Matemwe and offers comfortable rooms and suites, a swimming pool, and a range of activities, including kiteboarding, windsurfing, and fishing.

Matemwe Guest House: This budget-friendly guesthouse is located in the heart of Matemwe and offers comfortable rooms and suites, a swimming pool, and a range of activities, including snorkeling, diving, and fishing.

Recommended Restaurants in Matemwe

The Beach House Restaurant: This restaurant is located on the beach in Matemwe and serves a wide range of international dishes, including seafood, meat dishes, and vegetarian options.

Matemwe Beach Restaurant: This restaurant is located on the beach in Matemwe and serves a wide range of traditional Zanzibari dishes, including seafood, meat dishes, and vegetarian options.

Matemwe Fish Market Restaurant: This restaurant is located at the Matemwe Fish Market and serves a wide range of fresh seafood dishes, including fish, lobster, and prawns.

Michamvi

Michamvi is a picturesque fishing village located on the southeast coast of Zanzibar. This charming village is known for its stunning beaches, crystal-clear waters, and vibrant coral reefs. Michamvi is a popular destination for travelers looking for a relaxing and peaceful getaway from the hustle and bustle of Stone Town.

Top Attractions in Michamvi

Michamvi Beach: Michamvi Beach is one of the most beautiful beaches in Zanzibar. The beach is lined with palm trees, and the crystal-clear waters are perfect for swimming, snorkeling, and diving.

Michamvi Peninsula: The Michamvi Peninsula is a stunning natural attraction that offers breathtaking views of the Indian Ocean. The peninsula is also home to a wide range of marine life, including dolphins, whales, and sea turtles.

Michamvi Kae Beach: Michamvi Kae Beach is a secluded beach that is located on the southern tip of the Michamvi Peninsula. The beach is known for its crystal-clear waters, powdery white sand, and vibrant coral reefs.

Michamvi Village Tour: The Michamvi Village Tour is a great way to experience the local culture and traditions of Michamvi. The tour takes you through the village, where you can see traditional homes, meet local residents, and learn about the history and customs of the area.

Fishing and Boat Trips: Michamvi is a fishing village, and there are plenty of opportunities to go fishing or take a boat trip to explore the surrounding waters.

Recommended Accommodation in Michamvi

Michamvi Beach Resort: This luxury resort is located on the beach in Michamvi and offers stunning views of the Indian Ocean. The resort features comfortable rooms and suites, a swimming pool, and a range of activities, including snorkeling, diving, and fishing.

Kae Beach Resort: This boutique resort is located on the beach in Michamvi Kae and offers comfortable rooms and suites, a swimming pool, and a range of activities, including snorkeling, diving, and kayaking.

Michamvi Guest House: This budget-friendly guesthouse is located in the heart of Michamvi and offers comfortable rooms and suites, a swimming pool, and a range of activities, including snorkeling, diving, and fishing.

Recommended Restaurants in Michamvi

The Beach House Restaurant: This restaurant is located on the beach in Michamvi and serves a wide range of international dishes, including seafood, meat dishes, and vegetarian options.

Michamvi Beach Restaurant: This restaurant is located on the beach in Michamvi and serves a wide range of traditional Zanzibari dishes, including seafood, meat dishes, and vegetarian options.

Kae Beach Restaurant: This restaurant is located on the beach in Michamvi Kae and serves a wide range of fresh seafood dishes, including fish, lobster, and prawns.

Kizimkazi

Kizimkazi is a picturesque fishing village located on the southern tip of Zanzibar. This charming village is known for its stunning beaches, crystal-clear waters, and vibrant coral reefs. Kizimkazi is a popular destination for travelers looking for a relaxing and adventurous getaway from the hustle and bustle of Stone Town.

Top Attractions in Kizimkazi

Dolphin Watching Tour: Kizimkazi is famous for its dolphin watching tours. Take a boat trip to the nearby waters and get up close and personal with these intelligent and playful creatures.

Kizimkazi Beach: Kizimkazi Beach is one of the most beautiful beaches in Zanzibar. The beach is lined with

palm trees, and the crystal-clear waters are perfect for swimming, snorkeling, and diving.

Kizimkazi Cave: The Kizimkazi Cave is a stunning natural attraction that is located just outside the village. The cave is home to a wide range of stalactites and stalagmites, and offers breathtaking views of the surrounding countryside.

Kizimkazi Village Tour: The Kizimkazi Village Tour is a great way to experience the local culture and traditions of Kizimkazi. The tour takes you through the village, where you can see traditional homes, meet local residents, and learn about the history and customs of the area.

Fishing and Boat Trips: Kizimkazi is a fishing village, and there are plenty of opportunities to go fishing or take a boat trip to explore the surrounding waters.

Recommended Accommodation in Kizimkazi

Kizimkazi Beach Resort: This luxury resort is located on the beach in Kizimkazi and offers stunning views of the Indian Ocean. The resort features comfortable rooms and suites, a swimming pool, and a range of activities, including snorkeling, diving, and fishing.

Dolphin Bay Resort: This boutique resort is located on the beach in Kizimkazi and offers comfortable rooms and suites, a swimming pool, and a range of activities, including dolphin watching tours, snorkeling, and diving.

Kizimkazi Guest House: This budget-friendly guesthouse is located in the heart of Kizimkazi and offers comfortable rooms and suites, a swimming pool, and a range of activities, including snorkeling, diving, and fishing.

Recommended Restaurants in Kizimkazi

The Beach House Restaurant: This restaurant is located on the beach in Kizimkazi and serves a wide range of international dishes, including seafood, meat dishes, and vegetarian options.

Dolphin Bay Restaurant: This restaurant is located at the Dolphin Bay Resort and serves a wide range of traditional Zanzibari dishes, including seafood, meat dishes, and vegetarian options.

Kizimkazi Fish Market Restaurant: This restaurant is located at the Kizimkazi Fish Market and serves a wide range of fresh seafood dishes, including fish, lobster, and prawns.

Bwejuu

Bwejuu is a picturesque fishing village located on the southeast coast of Zanzibar. This charming village is known for its stunning beaches, crystal-clear waters, and vibrant coral reefs. Bwejuu is a popular destination for travelers looking for a relaxing and peaceful getaway from the hustle and bustle of Stone Town.

Top Attractions in Bwejuu

Bwejuu Beach: Bwejuu Beach is one of the most beautiful beaches in Zanzibar. The beach is lined with palm trees, and the crystal-clear waters are perfect for swimming, snorkeling, and diving.

Paje Beach: Paje Beach is a stunning beach located just north of Bwejuu. The beach is known for its crystal-clear waters, powdery white sand, and vibrant coral reefs.

Dongwe Ocean View: The Dongwe Ocean View is a stunning viewpoint that offers breathtaking views of the Indian Ocean. The viewpoint is located on a cliff overlooking the ocean, and is a great spot to watch the sunset.

Bwejuu Village Tour: The Bwejuu Village Tour is a great way to experience the local culture and traditions of Bwejuu. The tour takes you through the village, where you can see traditional homes, meet local residents, and learn about the history and customs of the area.

Kiteboarding and Windsurfing: Bwejuu is a popular destination for kiteboarders and windsurfers, with consistent winds and flat waters making it an ideal spot for these sports.

Recommended Accommodation in Bwejuu

Bwejuu Beach Resort: This luxury resort is located on the beach in Bwejuu and offers stunning views of the Indian Ocean. The resort features comfortable rooms and suites, a swimming pool, and a range of activities, including snorkeling, diving, and fishing.

Dongwe Ocean View Resort: This boutique resort is located on a cliff overlooking the Indian Ocean and offers stunning views of the ocean. The resort features comfortable rooms and suites, a swimming pool, and a range of activities, including kiteboarding, windsurfing, and fishing.

Bwejuu Guest House: This budget-friendly guesthouse is located in the heart of Bwejuu and offers comfortable rooms and suites, a swimming pool, and a range of activities, including snorkeling, diving, and fishing.

Recommended Restaurants in Bwejuu

The Beach House Restaurant: This restaurant is located on the beach in Bwejuu and serves a wide range of international dishes, including seafood, meat dishes, and vegetarian options.

Dongwe Ocean View Restaurant: This restaurant is located at the Dongwe Ocean View Resort and serves a wide range of traditional Zanzibari dishes, including seafood, meat dishes, and vegetarian options.

Bwejuu Fish Market Restaurant: This restaurant is located at the Bwejuu Fish Market and serves a wide range of fresh seafood dishes, including fish, lobster, and prawns.

Pongwe

Pongwe is a picturesque beach town located on the east coast of Zanzibar. This charming town is known for its stunning beaches, crystal-clear waters, and vibrant coral reefs. Pongwe is a popular destination for travelers looking for a relaxing and peaceful getaway from the hustle and bustle of Stone Town.

Top Attractions in Pongwe

Pongwe Beach: Pongwe Beach is one of the most beautiful beaches in Zanzibar. The beach is lined with

palm trees, and the crystal-clear waters are perfect for swimming, snorkeling, and diving.

Pongwe Bay: Pongwe Bay is a stunning natural attraction that is located just north of Pongwe. The bay is home to a wide range of marine life, including dolphins, whales, and sea turtles.

Pongwe Forest Reserve: The Pongwe Forest Reserve is a stunning natural attraction that is located just inland from Pongwe. The reserve is home to a wide range of flora and fauna, including monkeys, birds, and butterflies.

Pongwe Village Tour: The Pongwe Village Tour is a great way to experience the local culture and traditions of Pongwe. The tour takes you through the village, where you can see traditional homes, meet local residents, and learn about the history and customs of the area.

Snorkeling and Diving: Pongwe is a popular destination for snorkeling and diving, with numerous coral reefs and shipwrecks located just off the coast.

Recommended Accommodation in Pongwe

Pongwe Beach Resort: This luxury resort is located on the beach in Pongwe and offers stunning views of the Indian Ocean. The resort features comfortable rooms and suites, a swimming pool, and a range of activities, including snorkeling, diving, and fishing.

Pongwe Bay Resort: This boutique resort is located on the beach in Pongwe Bay and offers stunning views of the ocean. The resort features comfortable rooms and suites, a swimming pool, and a range of activities, including snorkeling, diving, and kayaking.

Pongwe Guest House: This budget-friendly guesthouse is located in the heart of Pongwe and offers comfortable rooms and suites, a swimming pool, and a range of activities, including snorkeling, diving, and fishing.

Recommended Restaurants in Pongwe

The Beach House Restaurant: This restaurant is located on the beach in Pongwe and serves a wide range of international dishes, including seafood, meat dishes, and vegetarian options.

Pongwe Beach Restaurant: This restaurant is located on the beach in Pongwe and serves a wide range of traditional Zanzibari dishes, including seafood, meat dishes, and vegetarian options.

Pongwe Fish Market Restaurant: This restaurant is located at the Pongwe Fish Market and serves a wide range of fresh seafood dishes, including fish, lobster, and prawns.

Chapter 5 • Zanzibari Cuisine and Food Experiences

Introduction to Zanzibari Cuisine

Zanzibar's cuisine is a reflection of its rich cultural heritage, with influences from African, Arabic, Indian, and European traditions. The island's cuisine is characterized by the use of fresh seafood, coconut milk, and a blend of spices that add depth and complexity to its dishes.

Staple Ingredients in Zanzibari Cuisine

Fresh seafood: Zanzibar is surrounded by coral reefs, making it an ideal location for fishing. Fresh seafood is a staple in Zanzibari cuisine, with popular dishes including grilled fish, seafood stews, and fish soups.

Coconut milk: Coconut milk is a common ingredient in Zanzibari cuisine, adding creaminess and richness to dishes such as curries and stews.

Spices: Zanzibar is famous for its spices, including cinnamon, cardamom, and cloves. These spices add depth and complexity to Zanzibari dishes, and are often used in combination with other ingredients to create unique flavor profiles.

Rice: Rice is a staple food in Zanzibar, often served with stews, curries, and other dishes.

Matooke: Matooke is a staple food in Zanzibar, made from steamed or boiled green bananas. It is often served with vegetables, meat, or beans.

Dining in Zanzibar

Dining in Zanzibar is a unique and enjoyable experience. Many restaurants in Zanzibar offer a range of traditional and international dishes, often made with fresh seafood and locally-sourced ingredients. Some popular dining spots in Zanzibar include:

Forodhani Night Food Market: A bustling night market in Stone Town that offers a range of traditional Zanzibari dishes, including urojo, nyama choma, and mandazi.

Darajani Market: A bustling market in Stone Town that offers a range of fresh produce, including fruits, vegetables, and seafood.

Beachfront restaurants: Many restaurants in Zanzibar are located on the beach, offering stunning views of the ocean and a range of seafood dishes.

Tips for Eating in Zanzibar

Be adventurous: Zanzibari cuisine is unique and flavorful, so be sure to try some of the local dishes.

Eat at local restaurants: Local restaurants in Zanzibar offer a range of traditional dishes at affordable prices.

Try street food: Street food in Zanzibar is delicious and affordable, with popular dishes including mandazi, urojo, and nyama choma.

Drink plenty of water: Zanzibar can be hot and humid, so be sure to drink plenty of water throughout the day.

Respect local customs: Zanzibar is a conservative island, so be sure to respect local customs and traditions when eating in public.

Famous Zanzibari Dishes

Below are some of the most famous Zanzibar dishes that you should try when visiting the island:

Urojo: A spicy soup made with fish, coconut milk, and a blend of spices. Urojo is a staple dish in Zanzibar and is often served with rice or chapati.

Nyama Choma: A popular dish made with grilled meat (usually goat or beef), served with vegetables and ugali (a staple food made from cornmeal or cassava flour). Nyama Choma is a favorite among locals and visitors alike.

Mandazi: Fried doughnuts that are often sprinkled with sugar or coated in chocolate. Mandazi is a popular snack in Zanzibar and is often served with a cup of coffee or tea.

Zanzibari Biryani: A flavorful rice dish made with a blend of spices, meat or seafood, and vegetables. Zanzibari Biryani is a staple dish in Zanzibar and is often served at special occasions.

Matooke: Steamed or boiled green bananas, often served with vegetables, meat, or beans. Matooke is a staple food in Zanzibar and is often served with a side of vegetables or meat.

Pilau: A flavorful rice dish made with a blend of spices, meat or seafood, and vegetables. Pilau is a popular dish in Zanzibar and is often served at special occasions.

Chapati: A type of flatbread that is popular in Zanzibar. Chapati is often served with a variety of fillings, including meat, vegetables, and beans.

Mchuzi wa Samaki: A fish stew made with a blend of spices, fish, and vegetables. Mchuzi wa Samaki is a popular dish in Zanzibar and is often served with rice or chapati.

Kaimati: Fried dough balls that are often sprinkled with sugar or coated in chocolate. Kaimati is a popular snack in Zanzibar and is often served with a cup of coffee or tea.

Mandazi ya Maji: Fried doughnuts that are made with a special type of flour that is only found in Zanzibar. Mandazi ya Maji is a popular snack in Zanzibar and is often served with a cup of coffee or tea.

Famous Zanzibari Drinks

Traditional Drinks

Fresh Coconut Water: Fresh coconut water is a staple drink in Zanzibar, and is often served as a refreshing welcome drink at hotels and restaurants.

Kahawa: Kahawa is a traditional Zanzibari coffee that is made from locally-grown coffee beans. It's strong, rich, and perfect for those looking for a caffeine boost.

Chai: Chai is a popular tea drink in Zanzibar, made with black tea, milk, and a blend of spices. It's a comforting and delicious drink that's perfect for any time of day.

Fresh Juices and Smoothies

Mango Juice: Fresh mango juice is a popular drink in Zanzibar, made from locally-grown mangoes. It's sweet, refreshing, and perfect for hot days.

Pineapple Juice: Fresh pineapple juice is another popular drink in Zanzibar, made from locally-grown pineapples. It's sweet, tangy, and perfect for those looking for a refreshing drink.

Coconut Smoothie: Coconut smoothies are a popular drink in Zanzibar, made with fresh coconut milk, fruit, and a blend of spices. They're creamy, refreshing, and perfect for hot days.

Local Beers and Spirits

Tusker Beer: Tusker beer is a popular beer in Zanzibar, brewed in Tanzania and perfect for those looking for a cold beer on a hot day.

Konyagi: Konyagi is a local spirit made from sugarcane or coconut sap. It's strong, flavorful, and often enjoyed with friends and family.

Zanzibar Gin: Zanzibar gin is a popular spirit made from locally-grown botanicals. It's flavorful, refreshing, and perfect for those looking for a unique drinking experience.

Other Popular Drinks

Fresh Sugarcane Juice: Fresh sugarcane juice is a popular drink in Zanzibar, made from locally-grown sugarcane. It's sweet, refreshing, and perfect for hot days.

Tamarind Juice: Tamarind juice is a popular drink in Zanzibar, made from locally-grown tamarind fruit. It's sour, sweet, and perfect for those looking for a unique drinking experience.

Ginger Beer: Ginger beer is a popular drink in Zanzibar, made from locally-grown ginger. It's spicy, refreshing, and perfect for those looking for a unique drinking experience.

Wine and Food Pairing

Understanding Zanzibari Cuisine

Before we dive into wine and food pairing, it's essential to understand the basics of Zanzibari cuisine. Zanzibari dishes are known for their bold flavors, aromas, and spices, which are often combined with fresh seafood, coconut milk, and rice. Some popular Zanzibari dishes include urojo (a spicy fish soup), nyama choma (grilled meat), and mandazi (fried doughnuts).

Wine and Food Pairing Tips

Below are some general wine and food pairing tips to keep in mind when dining in Zanzibar:

- Match the weight of the wine to the weight of the dish: A light and delicate dish like grilled fish or seafood requires a light and crisp wine, while a rich and heavy dish like nyama choma requires a full-bodied wine with high tannins.

- Consider the flavor profile of the dish: A dish with bold and spicy flavors like urojo requires a wine with a similar flavor profile, such as a spicy and full-bodied red wine.

- Don't forget about the role of acidity: A wine with high acidity can help cut through the richness of a dish like nyama choma, while a wine with low acidity can complement the delicate flavors of a dish like grilled fish.

Wine and Food Pairing Recommendations

Below are some specific wine and food pairing recommendations for popular Zanzibari dishes:

Urojo (Spicy Fish Soup): Pair with a spicy and full-bodied red wine like Shiraz or Syrah, which can complement the bold flavors of the dish.

Nyama Choma (Grilled Meat): Pair with a full-bodied red wine with high tannins like Cabernet Sauvignon or Merlot, which can complement the richness of the dish.

Mandazi (Fried Doughnuts): Pair with a sweet and sparkling wine like Moscato or Asti, which can complement the sweetness of the doughnuts.

Grilled Fish or Seafood: Pair with a light and crisp white wine like Sauvignon Blanc or Pinot Grigio, which can complement the delicate flavors of the dish.

Wine Bars and Restaurants in Zanzibar

The Rock Restaurant: Located in the heart of Stone Town, The Rock Restaurant offers an excellent selection of wines and delicious seafood dishes.

The Tea House Restaurant: Located in the historic Stone Town, The Tea House Restaurant offers an excellent selection of wines and delicious international dishes.

The Zanzibar Wine Bar: Located in the heart of Stone Town, The Zanzibar Wine Bar offers an excellent selection of wines from around the world, along with delicious snacks and small plates.

Culinary Experiences and Cooking Classes

Below are some culinary experiences and cooking classes that you can enjoy in Zanzibar, to help you discover the secrets of the island's delicious cuisine.

Cooking Classes in Zanzibar

Zanzibar Cooking School: Located in the heart of Stone Town, the Zanzibar Cooking School offers a range of cooking classes and workshops that focus on traditional Zanzibari cuisine.

Spice Island Cooking School: Located in a picturesque village on the outskirts of Stone Town, the Spice Island Cooking School offers a range of cooking classes and workshops that focus on traditional Zanzibari cuisine and cooking techniques.

Karama Cooking Class: Located in a local village on the outskirts of Stone Town, the Karama Cooking Class offers a range of cooking classes and workshops that focus on traditional Zanzibari cuisine and cooking techniques.

Culinary Experiences in Zanzibar

Spice Tour: Zanzibar is famous for its spices, and a spice tour is a great way to learn about the island's spice industry and see how spices are grown and harvested.

Fish Market Tour: The fish market in Stone Town is a bustling and colorful place, and a fish market tour is a great way to see the fresh seafood that is available in Zanzibar.

Food Tour: A food tour is a great way to sample the delicious cuisine of Zanzibar and learn about the island's food culture.

Dinner at a Local Restaurant: Dining at a local restaurant is a great way to experience the delicious cuisine of Zanzibar and learn about the island's food culture.

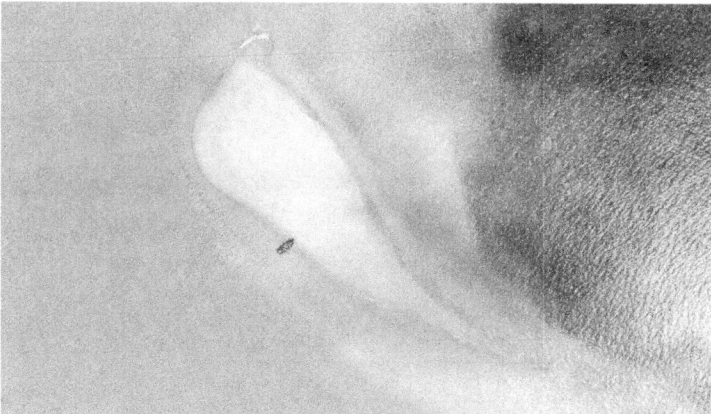

Chapter 6 • Outdoor Activities and Entertainment in Zanzibar

Snorkeling and Scuba diving in Zanzibar

Best Snorkeling and Scuba Diving Spots in Zanzibar

Mnemba Island: Located off the coast of Zanzibar, Mnemba Island is a popular snorkeling and scuba diving spot known for its crystal-clear waters, coral reefs, and diverse marine life.

Nungwi Reef: Located on the northwest coast of Zanzibar, Nungwi Reef is a popular snorkeling and scuba diving spot known for its coral reefs, sea turtles, and colorful fish.

Tumbatu Island: Located off the coast of Zanzibar, Tumbatu Island is a popular snorkeling and scuba diving spot known for its crystal-clear waters, coral reefs, and diverse marine life.

Kendwa Reef: Located on the northwest coast of Zanzibar, Kendwa Reef is a popular snorkeling and scuba diving spot known for its coral reefs, sea turtles, and colorful fish.

Snorkeling and Scuba Diving Operators in Zanzibar

Zanzibar Dive Center: Located in Stone Town, Zanzibar Dive Center is a popular snorkeling and scuba diving operator that offers a range of services and packages, including snorkeling and scuba diving trips, equipment rentals, and certification courses.

Mnemba Island Dive Center: Located on Mnemba Island, Mnemba Island Dive Center is a popular snorkeling and scuba diving operator that offers a range of services and packages, including snorkeling and scuba diving trips, equipment rentals, and certification courses.

Nungwi Dive Center: Located in Nungwi, Nungwi Dive Center is a popular snorkeling and scuba diving operator that offers a range of services and packages, including snorkeling and scuba diving trips, equipment rentals, and certification courses.

Tips and Essentials for Snorkeling and Scuba Diving in Zanzibar

- Respect the marine environment: Zanzibar's coral reefs and marine life are fragile and vulnerable to damage. Be sure to respect the marine environment and avoid touching or standing on coral reefs.

- Dive with a certified operator: Zanzibar has numerous snorkeling and scuba diving operators, but not all of them are certified or reputable. Be sure to dive with a certified operator to ensure your safety and the quality of your diving experience.

- Bring sunscreen and a hat: Zanzibar's sun can be intense, especially when snorkeling or scuba diving. Be sure to bring sunscreen and a hat to protect yourself from the sun.

- Learn about the local marine life: Zanzibar's coral reefs and marine life are fascinating and diverse. Be sure to learn about the local marine life and respect their habitats and behaviors.

Sandbank picnics

What is a Sandbank Picnic?

A sandbank picnic is a unique dining experience where you are taken to a secluded sandbank in the middle of the ocean, where a delicious meal is set up for you. The sandbank is usually surrounded by crystal-clear waters and coral reefs, making it a perfect spot for snorkeling, swimming, and relaxing.

How to Book a Sandbank Picnic in Zanzibar

Booking a sandbank picnic in Zanzibar is easy. You can book through a local tour operator or a hotel. Most tour operators and hotels offer sandbank picnic packages that include transportation, food, and drinks. You can also customize your picnic to suit your preferences and budget.

What to Expect from a Sandbank Picnic in Zanzibar

Below is what you can expect from a sandbank picnic in Zanzibar:

Transportation: You will be picked up from your hotel and taken to the sandbank by boat.

Food and Drinks: A delicious meal will be set up for you on the sandbank, including a variety of seafood, meat, and vegetarian options.

Snorkeling and Swimming: The sandbank is usually surrounded by crystal-clear waters and coral reefs, making it a perfect spot for snorkeling and swimming.

Relaxation: The sandbank is a secluded and peaceful spot, making it perfect for relaxation and sunbathing.

Best Time for a Sandbank Picnic in Zanzibar

The best time for a sandbank picnic in Zanzibar is during the dry season, which runs from June to October.

The weather is usually calm and sunny during this time, making it perfect for a sandbank picnic.

Dolphin tours

Best Time for Dolphin Tours in Zanzibar

The best time for dolphin tours in Zanzibar is during the dry season, which runs from June to October. The weather is usually calm and sunny during this time, making it perfect for a dolphin tour.

Types of Dolphins Found in Zanzibar

Bottlenose Dolphins: These are the most common species of dolphins found in Zanzibar. They are known for their playful and curious nature.

Spinner Dolphins: These dolphins are known for their acrobatic leaps and spins. They are commonly found in the waters around Zanzibar.

Humpback Dolphins: These dolphins are known for their distinctive hump on their back. They are commonly found in the waters around Zanzibar.

Dolphin Tour Operators in Zanzibar

Zanzibar Dolphin Tours: This operator offers a range of dolphin tours, including half-day and full-day tours.

Dolphin Adventures Zanzibar: This operator offers a range of dolphin tours, including snorkeling and swimming with dolphins.

Kizimkazi Dolphin Tours: This operator offers a range of dolphin tours, including half-day and full-day tours.

What to Expect from a Dolphin Tour in Zanzibar

Early Morning Departure: Dolphin tours in Zanzibar usually depart early in the morning, around 6:00 am.

Boat Ride: You will take a boat ride to the dolphin watching area, which is usually located in the waters around Kizimkazi.

Dolphin Watching: Once you arrive at the dolphin watching area, you will have the opportunity to see dolphins up close. You may even have the chance to swim with them.

Snorkeling and Swimming: Many dolphin tours in Zanzibar offer snorkeling and swimming opportunities, allowing you to explore the underwater world of the Indian Ocean.

Spice farm tours

History of Spice Trade in Zanzibar

Zanzibar's spice trade dates back to the 16th century, when the island was a major trading hub for spices, including cloves, cinnamon, cardamom, and nutmeg. The spice trade played a significant role in the island's economy and culture, and today, Zanzibar is still known for its high-quality spices.

What to Expect from a Spice Farm Tour in Zanzibar

Guided Tour: A knowledgeable guide will take you through the spice farm, explaining the different types of spices, how they are grown and harvested, and how they are used in traditional Zanzibari cuisine.

Spice Plantations: You will have the opportunity to see the different spice plantations, including clove, cinnamon, cardamom, and nutmeg.

Spice Processing: You will learn about the different methods of spice processing, including drying, grinding, and packaging.

Tasting and Shopping: Many spice farms offer the opportunity to taste and buy the different spices, as well as other local products, such as teas, coffees, and handicrafts.

Best Spice Farms to Visit in Zanzibar

Kizimbani Spice Farm: Located in the central region of Zanzibar, Kizimbani Spice Farm is one of the largest and most famous spice farms in the island.

Kidichi Spice Farm: Located in the northern region of Zanzibar, Kidichi Spice Farm is a popular destination for spice farm tours.

Mkoani Spice Farm: Located in the southern region of Zanzibar, Mkoani Spice Farm is a small, family-owned spice farm that offers a unique and personalized experience.

Sunset dhow cruises

What is a Dhow?

A dhow is a traditional Arabian sailing vessel that has been used for centuries to navigate the waters of the Indian Ocean. Dhows are characterized by their triangular sails and wooden hulls, and are often decorated with intricate carvings and colorful fabrics.

What to Expect from a Sunset Dhow Cruise in Zanzibar

Departure: The dhow cruise usually departs from Stone Town or one of the nearby beaches, and sets sail into the Indian Ocean.

Sailing: As the dhow sails through the calm waters of the Indian Ocean, you can relax and enjoy the stunning views of the Zanzibari coastline.

Snorkeling and Swimming: Many dhow cruises offer the opportunity to snorkel or swim in the crystal-clear waters of the Indian Ocean.

Sunset: As the sun begins to set, the dhow will anchor in a secluded spot, where you can watch the sunset in peace and tranquility.

Dinner and Drinks: Many dhow cruises offer a delicious seafood dinner and refreshing drinks, which you can enjoy while watching the sunset.

Best Time for a Sunset Dhow Cruise in Zanzibar

The best time for a sunset dhow cruise in Zanzibar is during the dry season, which runs from June to October. The weather is usually calm and sunny during this time, making it perfect for a dhow cruise.

Best Dhow Cruise Operators in Zanzibar

Zanzibar Dhow Cruises: This operator offers a range of dhow cruises, including sunset cruises, snorkeling cruises, and fishing cruises.

Dhow Safari: This operator offers a range of dhow cruises, including sunset cruises, snorkeling cruises, and fishing cruises.

Safari Blue: This operator offers a range of dhow cruises, including sunset cruises, snorkeling cruises, and fishing cruises.

Swimming with turtles

Best Places to Swim with Turtles in Zanzibar

Baraka Aquarium: Located in the southern part of the island, Baraka Aquarium is a popular spot for swimming with turtles.

Prison Island: Located off the coast of Stone Town, Prison Island is a popular spot for swimming with turtles and snorkeling.

Turtle Bay: Located on the eastern coast of the island, Turtle Bay is a secluded and peaceful spot for swimming with turtles.

What to Expect from Swimming with Turtles in Zanzibar

Guided Tour: A knowledgeable guide will take you to the best spots for swimming with turtles and provide you with information about these amazing creatures.

Snorkeling Equipment: You will be provided with snorkeling equipment, including masks, snorkels, and fins.

Swimming with Turtles: You will have the opportunity to swim with turtles in their natural habitat, getting up close and personal with these gentle creatures.

Relaxation: After swimming with turtles, you can relax on the beach or on the boat, enjoying the stunning views of the Indian Ocean.

Best Time for Swimming with Turtles in Zanzibar

The best time for swimming with turtles in Zanzibar is during the dry season, which runs from June to October. The weather is usually calm and sunny during this time, making it perfect for swimming with turtles.

Deep-sea fishing in Zanzibar

Best Time for Deep Sea Fishing in Zanzibar

The best time for deep sea fishing in Zanzibar is during the dry season, which runs from June to October. The weather is usually calm and sunny during this time, making it perfect for deep sea fishing.

Types of Fish Found in Zanzibar

Marlin: Marlin are one of the most prized game fish in Zanzibar, and can be found in the waters around the island.

Sailfish: Sailfish are another popular game fish in Zanzibar, and can be found in the waters around the island.

Tuna: Tuna are a common catch in Zanzibar, and can be found in the waters around the island.

Barracuda: Barracuda are a popular game fish in Zanzibar, and can be found in the waters around the island.

Deep Sea Fishing Operators in Zanzibar

Zanzibar Fishing Charters: This operator offers a range of deep sea fishing charters, including half-day and full-day trips.

Deep Sea Fishing Zanzibar: This operator offers a range of deep sea fishing trips, including half-day and full-day trips.

Fishing in Zanzibar: This operator offers a range of deep sea fishing trips, including half-day and full-day trips.

What to Expect from a Deep Sea Fishing Trip in Zanzibar

Departure: The deep sea fishing trip usually departs from Stone Town or one of the nearby beaches.

Fishing Gear: You will be provided with fishing gear, including rods, reels, and bait.

Fishing: You will have the opportunity to fish for a variety of species, including marlin, sailfish, tuna, and barracuda.

Lunch and Refreshments: You will be provided with lunch and refreshments, including soft drinks, beer, and snacks.

Safari Blue tours

What is Safari Blue?

Safari Blue is a full-day tour that takes you to the most beautiful and secluded islands in the Indian Ocean. The tour is designed to provide you with an unforgettable experience, combining snorkeling, swimming, and relaxation with stunning scenery and delicious seafood.

What to Expect from a Safari Blue Tour in Zanzibar

Departure: The tour usually departs from Fumba, a small fishing village located on the southwestern tip of Zanzibar.

Sailing: You will sail on a traditional Zanzibari dhow, a beautiful and comfortable sailing vessel that is perfect for exploring the Indian Ocean.

Snorkeling and Swimming: You will have the opportunity to snorkel and swim in the crystal-clear waters of the Indian Ocean, exploring the coral reefs and marine life of the area.

Seafood Lunch: You will enjoy a delicious seafood lunch on one of the secluded islands, featuring a variety of fresh seafood dishes and refreshing drinks.

Relaxation: After lunch, you will have the opportunity to relax on the beach or on the dhow, enjoying the stunning scenery and peaceful atmosphere of the Indian Ocean.

Best Time for a Safari Blue Tour in Zanzibar

The best time for a Safari Blue tour in Zanzibar is during the dry season, which runs from June to October. The weather is usually calm and sunny during this time, making it perfect for sailing and snorkeling.

Cultural village tours

What to Expect from a Cultural Village Tour in Zanzibar

Guided Tour: A knowledgeable guide will take you on a tour of the village, introducing you to the local people and explaining their customs and traditions.

Village Life: You will have the opportunity to see village life up close, including traditional houses, farms, and markets.

Local Cuisine: You will have the opportunity to try local cuisine, including traditional dishes such as ugali, sukuma wiki, and matooke.

Traditional Music and Dance: You will have the opportunity to experience traditional music and dance, including the famous Taarab music and dance.

Best Cultural Village Tours in Zanzibar

Jambiani Village Tour: Jambiani is a small fishing village located on the southeastern coast of Zanzibar. The village is known for its beautiful beaches, coral reefs, and traditional fishing practices.

Kizimkazi Village Tour: Kizimkazi is a small village located on the southwestern coast of Zanzibar. The village is known for its beautiful beaches, coral reefs, and traditional fishing practices.

Nungwi Village Tour: Nungwi is a small fishing village located on the northern tip of Zanzibar. The village is known for its beautiful beaches, coral reefs, and traditional fishing practices.

Jozani Forest tours

What is the Jozani Forest?

The Jozani Forest is a 2,500-hectare forest reserve that is home to a wide variety of flora and fauna. The forest is located in the center of Zanzibar, about 35 kilometers southeast of Stone Town. The Jozani Forest is a unique ecosystem that is characterized by a mix of tropical rainforest and coral rag forest.

What to Expect from a Jozani Forest Tour in Zanzibar

Guided Tour: A knowledgeable guide will take you on a tour of the forest, introducing you to the different types of flora and fauna that can be found there.

Wildlife Viewing: The Jozani Forest is home to a wide variety of wildlife, including red colobus monkeys, bushbabies, and over 100 species of birds.

Forest Walks: You will have the opportunity to take a guided walk through the forest, exploring the different types of vegetation and learning about the medicinal properties of the plants.

Picnic Lunch: Many Jozani Forest tours include a picnic lunch, which is usually served in a scenic spot within the forest.

Best Time for a Jozani Forest Tour in Zanzibar

The best time for a Jozani Forest tour in Zanzibar is during the dry season, which runs from June to October. The weather is usually calm and sunny during this time, making it perfect for forest walks and wildlife viewing.

Theatres, cinemas, and concerts

Theatres in Zanzibar

Old Fort Theatre: Located in Stone Town, the Old Fort Theatre is a historic venue that hosts a range of performances, including traditional taarab music and modern plays.

Mtoni Marine Theatre: Located in Mtoni, the Mtoni Marine Theatre is a popular venue for traditional and modern performances, including music, dance, and theatre.

Zanzibar Cultural Centre: Located in Stone Town, the Zanzibar Cultural Centre is a hub for cultural activities, including theatre performances, music concerts, and art exhibitions.

Cinemas in Zanzibar

Cine Afrique: Located in Stone Town, Cine Afrique is one of the oldest cinemas in Zanzibar, showing a range of films, including Hollywood blockbusters and local productions.

Zanzibar Cinema: Located in Stone Town, Zanzibar Cinema is a modern cinema that shows a range of films, including Hollywood blockbusters and local productions.

Mtoni Cinema: Located in Mtoni, Mtoni Cinema is a popular cinema that shows a range of films, including Hollywood blockbusters and local productions.

Concerts in Zanzibar

Zanzibar International Film Festival: Held annually in July, the Zanzibar International Film Festival is a popular event that showcases a range of films, including local and international productions.

Sauti za Busara: Held annually in February, Sauti za Busara is a popular music festival that showcases a range of traditional and modern music from East Africa and beyond.

Zanzibar Music Festival: Held annually in December, the Zanzibar Music Festival is a popular event that showcases a range of traditional and modern music from Zanzibar and beyond.

Nightlife in Zanzibar

Bars and Clubs in Zanzibar

The Rock Restaurant and Bar: Located on a rocky outcrop in the sea, The Rock Restaurant and Bar is a popular spot for sunset cocktails and dinner.

Cafe Arabica: Located in Stone Town, Cafe Arabica is a cozy bar that serves a range of cocktails and coffee.

Tatu Bar and Restaurant: Located in Nungwi, Tatu Bar and Restaurant is a popular spot for live music and dancing.

Kendwa Rocks: Located in Kendwa, Kendwa Rocks is a popular beach bar that hosts live music and parties.

Live Music and Events in Zanzibar

Full Moon Party: Held every month at Kendwa Rocks, the Full Moon Party is a popular event that features live music, dancing, and fireworks.

Zanzibar International Film Festival: Held annually in July, the Zanzibar International Film Festival is a popular event that showcases a range of films, including local and international productions.

Sauti za Busara: Held annually in February, Sauti za Busara is a popular music festival that showcases a range of traditional and modern music from East Africa and beyond.

Tips and Essentials for Enjoying Nightlife in Zanzibar

Dress Code: Dress code is generally casual in Zanzibar, but it's a good idea to dress modestly when visiting bars and clubs in Stone Town.

Safety: Zanzibar is generally a safe island, but it's always a good idea to take precautions when out at night, especially if you're traveling alone.

Respect Local Customs: Respect local customs and traditions when enjoying nightlife in Zanzibar, especially during Ramadan.

Have Fun: Most importantly, have fun and enjoy the laid-back and vibrant nightlife scene in Zanzibar!

Wellness: Spas, Retreats, and Yoga

Spas in Zanzibar

The Spa at The Z Hotel: Located in Nungwi, The Spa at The Z Hotel offers a range of treatments, including massages, facials, and body wraps.

The Spa at La Gemma dell'Est: Located in Nungwi, The Spa at La Gemma dell'Est offers a range of treatments, including massages, facials, and body wraps.

The Spa at The Residence Zanzibar: Located in Kizimkazi, The Spa at The Residence Zanzibar offers a range of treatments, including massages, facials, and body wraps.

Yoga and Wellness Retreats in Zanzibar

Yoga House Zanzibar: Located in Nungwi, Yoga House Zanzibar offers a range of yoga classes and workshops, as well as meditation and wellness programs.

Zanzibar Yoga Retreats: Located in Kizimkazi, Zanzibar Yoga Retreats offers a range of yoga and wellness programs, including meditation, pranayama, and yoga philosophy.

The Wellness Retreat Zanzibar: Located in Nungwi, The Wellness Retreat Zanzibar offers a range of wellness programs, including yoga, meditation, and massage therapy.

Chapter 7 • Shopping in Zanzibar

Fashion and Luxury Shopping

Traditional African Textiles

Below are some of the best places to buy traditional African textiles in Zanzibar:

Darajani Market: Located in Stone Town, Darajani Market is a bustling marketplace that sells a wide range of traditional African textiles, including kanga and kitenge fabrics.

Kanga Alley: Located in Stone Town, Kanga Alley is a narrow street that is lined with shops selling traditional African textiles, including kanga and kitenge fabrics.

Zanzibar Curios and Souvenirs: Located in Stone Town, Zanzibar Curios and Souvenirs is a shop that sells a wide range of traditional African textiles, including kanga and kitenge fabrics.

Luxury Jewelry and Accessories

Zanzibar Gold and Silver: Located in Stone Town, Zanzibar Gold and Silver is a shop that sells a wide range of luxury jewelry and accessories, including gold and silver pieces, precious stones, and high-end watches.

Jafferji Jewellers: Located in Stone Town, Jafferji Jewellers is a shop that sells a wide range of luxury jewelry and accessories, including gold and silver pieces, precious stones, and high-end watches.

The Zanzibar Collection: Located in Stone Town, The Zanzibar Collection is a shop that sells a wide range of luxury jewelry and accessories, including gold and silver pieces, precious stones, and high-end watches.

High-End Fashion

The Zanzibar Boutique: Located in Stone Town, The Zanzibar Boutique is a shop that sells a wide range of high-end fashion items, including designer clothing and accessories, luxurious home decor items, and unique gifts.

La Petite Boutique: Located in Stone Town, La Petite Boutique is a shop that sells a wide range of high-end fashion items, including designer clothing and accessories, luxurious home decor items, and unique gifts.

The Gallery: Located in Stone Town, The Gallery is a shop that sells a wide range of high-end fashion items, including designer clothing and accessories, luxurious home decor items, and unique gifts.

Local Markets and Souvenirs

Local Markets in Zanzibar

Darajani Market: Located in Stone Town, Darajani Market is one of the largest and most bustling markets in Zanzibar, offering a wide range of goods, including fresh produce, spices, textiles, and handicrafts.

Slipway Market: Located in Stone Town, Slipway Market is a bustling marketplace that offers a wide range of goods, including fresh seafood, spices, textiles, and handicrafts.

Mwenge Market: Located in Mwenge, Mwenge Market is a bustling marketplace that offers a wide range of goods, including fresh produce, spices, textiles, and handicrafts.

Souvenirs in Zanzibar

Textiles and Fabrics: Zanzibar is famous for its colorful textiles and fabrics, including kanga and kitenge fabrics, which make perfect souvenirs.

Handicrafts and Woodcarvings: Zanzibar is home to a number of skilled artisans who create beautiful handicrafts and woodcarvings, including intricately carved wooden doors, chests, and masks.

Spices and Essential Oils: Zanzibar is famous for its fragrant spices and essential oils, including cloves, cinnamon, and lemongrass, which make perfect souvenirs.

Local Delicacies and Snacks: Zanzibar is home to a number of delicious local delicacies and snacks, including dried fruits, nuts, and spices, which make perfect souvenirs.

Artisan Crafts and Workshops

Traditional Crafts in Zanzibar

Woodcarving: Woodcarving is a traditional craft in Zanzibar, with artisans creating intricate and beautiful pieces from wood, including doors, chests, and masks.

Textiles: Textiles are a major part of Zanzibari culture, with artisans creating beautiful and colorful fabrics, including kanga and kitenge fabrics.

Pottery: Pottery is another traditional craft in Zanzibar, with artisans creating beautiful and functional pieces from clay, including pots, plates, and cups.

Artisan Workshops in Zanzibar

The Zanzibar Artisan Workshop: Located in Stone Town, The Zanzibar Artisan Workshop is a cooperative of local artisans who create traditional crafts, including woodcarvings, textiles, and pottery.

The Mwenge Woodcarvers' Village: Located in Mwenge, The Mwenge Woodcarvers' Village is a community of woodcarvers who create intricate and beautiful pieces from wood.

The Unguja Ukuu Pottery Workshop: Located in Unguja Ukuu, The Unguja Ukuu Pottery Workshop is a cooperative of local potters who create beautiful and functional pieces from clay.

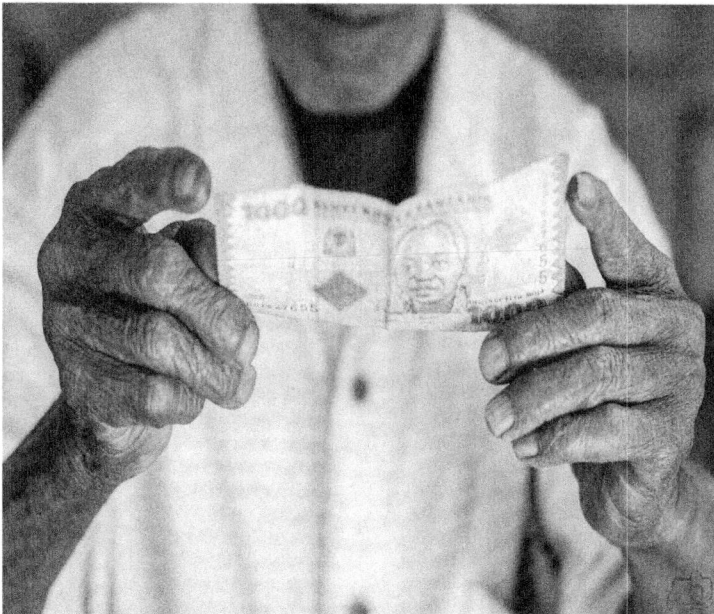

Chapter 8 • Practical Information

Health and Safety Tips

Health Tips

Vaccinations: Make sure you have all the necessary vaccinations before traveling to Zanzibar, including yellow fever, hepatitis A, and typhoid.

Malaria: Zanzibar is a malaria-endemic area, so make sure you take the necessary precautions, including taking antimalarial medication and using insecticide-treated bed nets.

Sun Protection: Zanzibar is a tropical island, and the sun can be intense. Make sure you wear sunscreen, a hat, and sunglasses to protect yourself from the sun.

Food and Water Safety: Make sure you eat at reputable restaurants and avoid eating undercooked meat or raw vegetables. Also, make sure you drink bottled or filtered water to avoid getting sick.

Safety Tips

Be Aware of Your Surroundings: Zanzibar is generally a safe island, but it's always a good idea to be aware of your surroundings, especially in crowded areas like markets and bus stations.

Use Licensed Taxis: Make sure you use licensed taxis or ride-sharing services to get around the island, as unlicensed taxis can be unreliable and even dangerous.

Avoid Carrying Large Amounts of Cash: Avoid carrying large amounts of cash, as this can make you a target for thieves and scammers. Instead, use credit cards or traveler's checks.

Respect Local Customs: Zanzibar is a conservative island, so make sure you respect local customs and traditions, especially when visiting mosques or other cultural sites.

Beach Safety

Swim at Patrolled Beaches: Make sure you swim at patrolled beaches, as these are generally safer than unpatrolled beaches.

Watch for Rip Currents: Watch for rip currents, which can be strong and unpredictable. If you get caught in a rip current, don't try to swim against it. Instead, swim parallel to the shore until you're out of the current.

Don't Swim at Night: Don't swim at night, as this can be dangerous due to the lack of visibility and the presence of marine life like sea urchins and jellyfish.

Protect Your Skin: Protect your skin from the sun and wind by wearing sunscreen, a hat, and sunglasses.

Emergency Contacts

Emergency Services

- Police: 999
- Ambulance: 999
- Fire Brigade: 999
- Coast Guard: 222 2121

Hospitals and Medical Facilities

Mnazi Mmoja Hospital: Located in Stone Town, Mnazi Mmoja Hospital is one of the largest and most well-equipped hospitals in Zanzibar.

Abeid Amane Karume Hospital: Located in Stone Town, Abeid Amane Karume Hospital is a modern hospital that offers a range of medical services, including emergency care, surgery, and maternity care.

Zanzibar Private Hospital: Located in Stone Town, Zanzibar Private Hospital is a private hospital that offers a range of medical services, including emergency care, surgery, and maternity care.

Embassies and Consulates

British High Commission: Located in Stone Town, the British High Commission is the diplomatic mission of the United Kingdom in Zanzibar.

American Embassy: Located in Dar es Salaam, the American Embassy is the diplomatic mission of the United States in Tanzania, and also provides assistance to American citizens in Zanzibar.

Canadian High Commission: Located in Dar es Salaam, the Canadian High Commission is the diplomatic mission of Canada in Tanzania, and also provides assistance to Canadian citizens in Zanzibar.

Insurance and Emergency Services

Travel Insurance: Make sure you have travel insurance that covers you for medical emergencies, trip cancellations, and delays.

Emergency Medical Evacuation: Make sure you have emergency medical evacuation coverage, which can help you get medical attention quickly in the event of an emergency.

24-Hour Emergency Assistance: Make sure you have 24-hour emergency assistance, which can provide you with help and support in the event of an emergency.

Communication and Internet Access

Mobile Phone Networks

Below are some of the top mobile phone networks in Zanzibar:

Vodacom: Vodacom is one of the largest mobile phone networks in Tanzania, with excellent coverage in Zanzibar.

Tigo: Tigo is another popular mobile phone network in Tanzania, with good coverage in Zanzibar.

Airtel: Airtel is a popular mobile phone network in Tanzania, with good coverage in Zanzibar.

Internet Access

Internet Cafes: Internet cafes are widely available in Zanzibar, with many located in Stone Town and other popular tourist areas.

Hotels and Resorts: Many hotels and resorts in Zanzibar offer Wi-Fi, making it easy to stay connected during your trip.

Restaurants and Cafes: Many restaurants and cafes in Zanzibar offer Wi-Fi, making it easy to stay connected while you eat and drink.

Postal Services

Zanzibar Post Office: Located in Stone Town, the Zanzibar Post Office is the main post office on the island.

Nungwi Post Office: Located in Nungwi, the Nungwi Post Office is a convenient option for tourists staying in the north of the island.

Kendwa Post Office: Located in Kendwa, the Kendwa Post Office is a convenient option for tourists staying in the northwest of the island.

Chapter 9 • Recommended Itineraries

One day in Zanzibar

Stop 1: Stone Town (9:00 am - 10:00 am)

Start your day by exploring Stone Town, the historic heart of Zanzibar. Wander through the narrow streets and alleys, taking in the sights and sounds of the bustling markets and bazaars.

Stop 2: Darajani Market (10:00 am - 11:30 am)

Visit the Darajani Market, one of the largest and most vibrant markets in Zanzibar. Here, you can find everything from fresh produce and spices to handicrafts and souvenirs.

Stop 3: Lunch at a Local Restaurant (11:30 am - 1:00 pm)

Take a break for lunch at a local restaurant, where you can try some of Zanzibar's delicious seafood and traditional dishes.

Stop 4: Prison Island (2:00 pm - 4:00 pm)

Take a boat trip to Prison Island, a small island located just off the coast of Stone Town. Here, you can see the historic prison buildings, as well as a variety of marine life, including sea turtles and colorful fish.

Stop 5: Sunset at the Beach (5:00 pm - 7:00 pm)

End your day with a sunset at one of Zanzibar's stunning beaches. Relax and enjoy the tranquil atmosphere, and take in the breathtaking views of the Indian Ocean.

Three days in Zanzibar

Day 1: Stone Town and the Beach

Stop 1: Stone Town (9:00 am - 12:00 pm)

Start your day by exploring Stone Town, the historic heart of Zanzibar. Wander through the narrow streets and alleys, taking in the sights and sounds of the bustling markets and bazaars.

Stop 2: Lunch at a Local Restaurant (12:00 pm - 1:30 pm)

Take a break for lunch at a local restaurant, where you can try some of Zanzibar's delicious seafood and traditional dishes.

Stop 3: Beach Relaxation (2:00 pm - 5:00 pm)

Spend the afternoon relaxing on one of Zanzibar's stunning beaches, such as Nungwi Beach or Kendwa Beach.

Day 2: Prison Island, the Spice Plantations, and Jozani Forest

Stop 1: Prison Island (9:00 am - 11:00 am)

Take a boat trip to Prison Island, a small island located just off the coast of Stone Town. Here, you can see the historic prison buildings, as well as a variety of marine life, including sea turtles and colorful fish.

Stop 2: Spice Plantations (11:30 am - 1:00 pm)

Visit one of Zanzibar's famous spice plantations, where you can learn about the history and production of spices, such as cloves, cinnamon, and nutmeg.

Stop 3: Jozani Forest (2:00 pm - 4:00 pm)

Explore the Jozani Forest, a beautiful and tranquil nature reserve that is home to a variety of wildlife, including monkeys, birds, and butterflies.

Day 3: North Coast and the Beach

Stop 1: Nungwi Village (9:00 am - 11:00 am)

Visit the Nungwi Village, a small fishing village located on the north coast of Zanzibar. Here, you can see the local fishermen at work, as well as the beautiful beaches and coral reefs.

Stop 2: Kendwa Beach (11:30 am - 1:00 pm)

Spend the morning relaxing on Kendwa Beach, one of Zanzibar's most beautiful and tranquil beaches.

Stop 3: Sunset Cruise (4:00 pm - 6:00 pm)

End your day with a sunset cruise, where you can watch the sunset over the Indian Ocean while enjoying snacks and drinks.

Five days in Zanzibar

Day 1: Stone Town and the Beach

Stop 1: Stone Town (9:00 am - 12:00 pm)

Start your day by exploring Stone Town, the historic heart of Zanzibar. Wander through the narrow streets and alleys, taking in the sights and sounds of the bustling markets and bazaars.

Stop 2: Lunch at a Local Restaurant (12:00 pm - 1:30 pm)

Take a break for lunch at a local restaurant, where you can try some of Zanzibar's delicious seafood and traditional dishes.

Stop 3: Beach Relaxation (2:00 pm - 5:00 pm)

Spend the afternoon relaxing on one of Zanzibar's stunning beaches, such as Nungwi Beach or Kendwa Beach.

Day 2: Prison Island, the Spice Plantations, and Jozani Forest

Stop 1: Prison Island (9:00 am - 11:00 am)

Take a boat trip to Prison Island, a small island located just off the coast of Stone Town. Here, you can see the historic prison buildings, as well as a variety of marine life, including sea turtles and colorful fish.

Stop 2: Spice Plantations (11:30 am - 1:00 pm)

Visit one of Zanzibar's famous spice plantations, where you can learn about the history and production of spices, such as cloves, cinnamon, and nutmeg.

Stop 3: Jozani Forest (2:00 pm - 4:00 pm)

Explore the Jozani Forest, a beautiful and tranquil nature reserve that is home to a variety of wildlife, including monkeys, birds, and butterflies.

Day 3: North Coast and the Beach

Stop 1: Nungwi Village (9:00 am - 11:00 am)

Visit the Nungwi Village, a small fishing village located on the north coast of Zanzibar. Here, you can see the local fishermen at work, as well as the beautiful beaches and coral reefs.

Stop 2: Kendwa Beach (11:30 am - 1:00 pm)

Spend the morning relaxing on Kendwa Beach, one of Zanzibar's most beautiful and tranquil beaches.

Stop 3: Sunset Cruise (4:00 pm - 6:00 pm)

End your day with a sunset cruise, where you can watch the sunset over the Indian Ocean while enjoying snacks and drinks.

Day 4: South Coast and the Beach

Stop 1: Kizimkazi Village (9:00 am - 11:00 am)

Visit the Kizimkazi Village, a small fishing village located on the south coast of Zanzibar. Here, you can see the local fishermen at work, as well as the beautiful beaches and coral reefs.

Stop 2: Menai Bay (11:30 am - 1:00 pm)

Take a boat trip to Menai Bay, a beautiful and tranquil bay that is home to a variety of marine life, including dolphins and sea turtles.

Stop 3: Beach Relaxation (2:00 pm - 5:00 pm)

Spend the afternoon relaxing on one of Zanzibar's stunning beaches, such as Kizimkazi Beach or Menai Beach.

Day 5: Stone Town and Departure

Stop 1: Stone Town (9:00 am - 12:00 pm)

Spend the morning exploring Stone Town, the historic heart of Zanzibar. Visit the local markets and bazaars, and take in the sights and sounds of the bustling streets.

Stop 2: Departure (12:00 pm - 2:00 pm)

End your trip with a departure from Zanzibar International Airport or the port of Stone Town.

Seven days in Zanzibar

Day 1: Arrival and Stone Town Exploration

Arrive in Zanzibar and spend the day exploring Stone Town, the historic heart of the island. Visit the local markets and bazaars, and take in the sights and sounds of the bustling streets.

Day 2: Prison Island and the Spice Plantations

Take a boat trip to Prison Island, a small island located just off the coast of Stone Town. Learn about the island's history and see the historic prison buildings. In the afternoon, visit one of Zanzibar's famous spice plantations, where you can learn about the history and production of spices.

Day 3: North Coast and the Beach

Spend the day relaxing on one of Zanzibar's stunning beaches, such as Nungwi Beach or Kendwa Beach. Take a boat trip to the nearby coral reefs, where you can snorkel or dive and see the incredible marine life.

Day 4: Jozani Forest and the South Coast

Explore the Jozani Forest, a beautiful and tranquil nature reserve that is home to a variety of wildlife, including monkeys, birds, and butterflies. In the afternoon, visit the south coast of the island, where you can relax on the beach and enjoy the stunning views.

Day 5: Menai Bay and the Dolphins

Take a boat trip to Menai Bay, a beautiful and tranquil bay that is home to a variety of marine life, including dolphins and sea turtles. Spend the day snorkeling or diving and enjoying the incredible scenery.

Day 6: Stone Town and the Night Market

Spend the day exploring Stone Town, the historic heart of the island. Visit the local markets and bazaars, and take in the sights and sounds of the bustling streets. In the evening, visit the night market, where you can try local food and drinks and buy souvenirs.

Day 7: Departure

Spend the morning relaxing on the beach or exploring Stone Town. Depart for the airport or port in the afternoon, bringing back memories of your incredible journey through Zanzibar.

Chapter 10 • Travelling with Children

Child-Friendly Attractions

Below are some of the top child-friendly attractions in Zanzibar:

Beaches

Nungwi Beach: Located on the north coast of Zanzibar, Nungwi Beach is a popular spot for families with kids. The beach is lined with restaurants, bars, and shops, and there are plenty of activities for kids to enjoy, including snorkeling, swimming, and building sandcastles.

Kendwa Beach: Located on the northwest coast of Zanzibar, Kendwa Beach is another popular spot for families with kids. The beach is known for its calm and clear waters, making it perfect for swimming and snorkeling.

Paje Beach: Located on the southeast coast of Zanzibar, Paje Beach is a popular spot for families with kids who love water sports. The beach is known for its strong winds, making it perfect for kiteboarding and windsurfing.

Water Parks and Pools

Zanzibar Water Park: Located in Stone Town, Zanzibar Water Park is a popular spot for families with kids. The park features several water slides, a swimming pool, and a playground for kids.

Mtoni Marine Water Park: Located in Mtoni, Mtoni Marine Water Park is a popular spot for families with kids who love water sports. The park features several water slides, a swimming pool, and a playground for kids.

National Parks and Reserves

Jozani Forest National Park: Located in the center of Zanzibar, Jozani Forest National Park is a popular spot for families with kids who love wildlife and nature. The park is home to several species of monkeys, including the rare red colobus monkey.

Menai Bay Conservation Area: Located on the south coast of Zanzibar, Menai Bay Conservation Area is a popular spot for families with kids who love dolphins and other marine life. The area is home to several species of dolphins, including the bottlenose dolphin.

Other Child-Friendly Attractions

Zanzibar Butterfly Centre: Located in Stone Town, Zanzibar Butterfly Centre is a popular spot for families with kids who love butterflies and other insects. The center is home to several species of butterflies, including the monarch butterfly.

Cheetah's Rock: Located in Stone Town, Cheetah's Rock is a popular spot for families with kids who love animals. The center is home to several species of animals, including cheetahs, lions, and monkeys.

Child-Friendly Accommodation

Below are some of the best child-friendly hotels and resorts in Zanzibar:

Luxury Resorts

The Z Hotel: Located in Nungwi, The Z Hotel is a luxurious resort that offers a range of child-friendly facilities, including a kids' club, a swimming pool, and a playground.

Essque Zalu Zanzibar: Located in Nungwi, Essque Zalu Zanzibar is a luxurious resort that offers a range of child-friendly facilities, including a kids' club, a swimming pool, and a playground.

Diamonds La Gemma dell'Est: Located in Nungwi, Diamonds La Gemma dell'Est is a luxurious resort that offers a range of child-friendly facilities, including a kids' club, a swimming pool, and a playground.

Mid-Range Hotels

Tanzanite Beach Resort: Located in Nungwi, Tanzanite Beach Resort is a mid-range hotel that offers a range of child-friendly facilities, including a swimming pool, a playground, and a kids' club.

Sazani Beach Hotel: Located in Nungwi, Sazani Beach Hotel is a mid-range hotel that offers a range of child-friendly facilities, including a swimming pool, a playground, and a kids' club.

Waridi Beach Resort: Located in Nungwi, Waridi Beach Resort is a mid-range hotel that offers a range of child-friendly facilities, including a swimming pool, a playground, and a kids' club.

Budget-Friendly Options

Paje Beach Bungalows: Located in Paje, Paje Beach Bungalows is a budget-friendly resort that offers a range of child-friendly facilities, including a swimming pool, a playground, and a kids' club.

Jambiani Beach Bungalows: Located in Jambiani, Jambiani Beach Bungalows is a budget-friendly resort that offers a range of child-friendly facilities, including a swimming pool, a playground, and a kids' club.

Kendwa Beach Bungalows: Located in Kendwa, Kendwa Beach Bungalows is a budget-friendly resort that offers a range of child-friendly facilities, including a swimming pool, a playground, and a kids' club.

Chapter 11 • Travelling on a Budget

Budget-Friendly Accommodation

Below are some of the top budget-friendly accommodation options in Zanzibar:

Hostels

Zanzibar Hostel: Located in Stone Town, Zanzibar Hostel is a popular option for backpackers and budget travelers. The hostel offers dorm rooms and private rooms, as well as a communal kitchen and lounge area.

Nungwi Hostel: Located in Nungwi, Nungwi Hostel is a great option for travelers looking for a relaxed and laid-back atmosphere. The hostel offers dorm rooms and private rooms, as well as a communal kitchen and lounge area.

Paje Hostel: Located in Paje, Paje Hostel is a popular option for travelers looking for a beachfront location. The hostel offers dorm rooms and private rooms, as well as a communal kitchen and lounge area.

Guesthouses

Zanzibar Guest House: Located in Stone Town, Zanzibar Guest House is a popular option for travelers looking for a comfortable and convenient location. The guesthouse offers private rooms and suites, as well as a communal kitchen and lounge area.

Nungwi Guest House: Located in Nungwi, Nungwi Guest House is a great option for travelers looking for a relaxed and laid-back atmosphere. The guesthouse offers private rooms and suites, as well as a communal kitchen and lounge area.

Paje Guest House: Located in Paje, Paje Guest House is a popular option for travelers looking for a beachfront location. The guesthouse offers private rooms and suites, as well as a communal kitchen and lounge area.

Budget-Friendly Resorts

Paje Beach Resort: Located in Paje, Paje Beach Resort is a popular option for travelers looking for a beachfront location. The resort offers private rooms and suites, as well as a communal kitchen and lounge area.

Nungwi Beach Resort: Located in Nungwi, Nungwi Beach Resort is a great option for travelers looking for a relaxed and laid-back atmosphere. The resort offers private rooms and suites, as well as a communal kitchen and lounge area.

Kendwa Beach Resort: Located in Kendwa, Kendwa Beach Resort is a popular option for travelers looking for a beachfront location. The resort offers private rooms and suites, as well as a communal kitchen and lounge area.

Cheap Eats and Local Food

Traditional Street Food

Street food is a staple of Zanzibari cuisine, and you can find a wide range of delicious and affordable options on the streets of Stone Town and other towns and villages. Below are some popular traditional street foods to try:

Mandazi: Fried doughnuts that are sprinkled with sugar and are a popular breakfast or snack item.

Mishkaki: Skewers of marinated meat (usually beef or chicken) that are grilled over an open flame.

Urojo: A traditional Zanzibari soup made with a variety of ingredients, including meat, vegetables, and spices.

Vitumbua: Fried rice cakes that are a popular snack item.

Local Restaurants

The Tea House Restaurant: Located in Stone Town, this restaurant serves a wide range of traditional Zanzibari dishes, including mishkaki and urojo.

The Old Fort Restaurant: Located in Stone Town, this restaurant serves a wide range of traditional Zanzibari dishes, including mandazi and vitumbua.

The Beach House Restaurant: Located in Nungwi, this restaurant serves a wide range of seafood dishes, including grilled fish and lobster.

Markets

Darajani Market: Located in Stone Town, this market is one of the largest and most vibrant in Zanzibar. You can find a wide range of fresh produce, spices, and other local ingredients.

Forodhani Night Market: Located in Stone Town, this market is a great place to find traditional Zanzibari street food, including mishkaki and urojo.

Nungwi Market: Located in Nungwi, this market is a great place to find fresh seafood and other local ingredients.

Free and Affordable Attractions

Below are some free and affordable attractions to explore in Zanzibar:

Free Attractions

Stone Town: Explore the narrow streets and alleys of Stone Town, the historic heart of Zanzibar. Take in the sights and sounds of the bustling markets and bazaars.

Nungwi Beach: Relax on the stunning beach of Nungwi, located on the north coast of Zanzibar. Enjoy the crystal-clear waters and powdery white sand.

Jozani Forest: Explore the Jozani Forest, a beautiful and tranquil nature reserve located in the center of Zanzibar. Take a self-guided tour of the forest and spot some of the island's unique wildlife.

Forodhani Night Market: Visit the Forodhani Night Market, a bustling market that takes place every evening in Stone Town. Try some of the local street food and drinks, and browse the stalls selling souvenirs and local handicrafts.

Affordable Attractions

Prison Island: Take a boat trip to Prison Island, a small island located just off the coast of Stone Town.

Learn about the island's history and see the historic prison buildings. (Cost: around $10-$15 per person)

Spice Plantations: Visit one of Zanzibar's famous spice plantations, where you can learn about the history and production of spices, such as cloves, cinnamon, and nutmeg. (Cost: around $5-$10 per person)

Zanzibar Butterfly Centre: Visit the Zanzibar Butterfly Centre, a beautiful and tranquil nature reserve located in the center of Zanzibar. See some of the island's unique butterfly species and learn about their habitat and behavior. (Cost: around $5-$10 per person)

Mtoni Marine Park: Visit the Mtoni Marine Park, a beautiful and tranquil nature reserve located on the west coast of Zanzibar. Take a snorkeling or diving trip to see some of the island's unique marine life. (Cost: around $20-$30 per person)

Transportation Tips for Saving Money

Below are some transportation tips for saving money in Zanzibar:

Using Public Transportation

Dala-Dala: Dala-dala is a local bus service that operates throughout the island. It's a cheap and convenient way to get around, with fares starting from as low as 500 Tanzanian shillings (around $0.20 USD).

Local Taxis: Local taxis are another affordable option for getting around Zanzibar. You can negotiate the fare with the driver before you start your journey.

Renting a Vehicle

Motorbikes: Renting a motorbike is a cheap and convenient way to get around Zanzibar. You can rent a motorbike for around 20,000-30,000 Tanzanian shillings (around $8-12 USD) per day.

Cars: Renting a car is another option for exploring Zanzibar. You can rent a car for around 50,000-70,000 Tanzanian shillings (around $20-28 USD) per day.

Walking and Cycling

Walking Tours: Take a walking tour of Stone Town and explore the narrow streets and alleys. You can take a self-guided tour or hire a local guide.

Cycling: Rent a bicycle and explore the island at your own pace. Cycling is a great way to see the sights and get some exercise at the same time.

Tips for Saving Money on Transportation

- Negotiate Fares: Always negotiate the fare with the driver before you start your journey.

- Use Public Transportation: Public transportation is a cheap and convenient way to get around Zanzibar.

- Rent a Vehicle for a Short Period: If you only need a vehicle for a short period, consider renting a motorbike or car for a day or two.

- Walk or Cycle: Walking and cycling are great ways to explore Zanzibar, especially in Stone Town and other urban areas.

Chapter 12 • Day Trips and Excursions

Prison Island (Changuu Island)

Located just off the coast of Stone Town, Prison Island is a popular day trip destination for travelers visiting Zanzibar. This small island has a rich history, stunning beaches, and a unique attraction that sets it apart from other islands in the archipelago.

History of Prison Island

Prison Island, also known as Changuu Island, has a fascinating history that dates back to the 19th century. The island was originally used as a quarantine station for yellow fever patients, but it was later converted into a prison colony. The prison was built in 1893 and was used to house rebellious slaves and prisoners from the mainland.

Attractions on Prison Island

The Prison Ruins: The prison ruins are the main attraction on the island. Visitors can explore the old prison cells, the courtyard, and the watchtower.

The Beach: Prison Island has a stunning beach with crystal-clear waters and powdery white sand. Visitors can relax on the beach, swim, or snorkel.

The Giant Tortoises: Prison Island is home to a group of giant tortoises that were brought to the island in the 19th century. Visitors can see these gentle giants up close and learn about their habitat and behavior.

How to Get to Prison Island

Take a Ferry from Stone Town: The ferry to Prison Island departs from the harbor in Stone Town. The ferry ride takes about 30 minutes and costs around 5,000-10,000 Tanzanian shillings (around $2-5 USD) per person, depending on the type of ferry and the time of day.

Take a Private Boat: Visitors can also take a private boat to Prison Island. This option is more expensive than taking the ferry, but it offers more flexibility and comfort.

Mnemba Atoll

Located just off the coast of Zanzibar, Mnemba Atoll is a stunning marine reserve that is perfect for a day trip. This picturesque atoll is known for its crystal-clear waters, white sandy beaches, and incredible marine life.

Below is a guide to visiting Mnemba Atoll as a day trip destination.

About Mnemba Atoll

Mnemba Atoll is a small, uninhabited island located about 3 kilometers off the coast of Zanzibar. The atoll is part of the Mnemba Marine Reserve, which is a protected area that is home to an incredible array of marine life. The atoll is surrounded by a coral reef, which makes it a popular spot for snorkeling and diving.

Attractions and Activities

Snorkeling and Diving: The coral reef surrounding Mnemba Atoll is home to an incredible array of marine life, including sea turtles, rays, and colorful fish.

Beach Relaxation: The atoll has several stunning beaches that are perfect for relaxation. Enjoy the sun, sand, and sea, and take a break from the hustle and bustle of everyday life.

Swimming and Swimming with Dolphins: The waters surrounding Mnemba Atoll are home to a pod of bottlenose dolphins. Take a swim with these incredible creatures and experience the thrill of a lifetime.

Picnicking and BBQs: The atoll has several picnic areas and BBQ facilities, making it the perfect spot for a family day out or a romantic picnic.

How to Get to Mnemba Atoll

Take a Boat from Nungwi: The most common way to get to Mnemba Atoll is by taking a boat from Nungwi. The boat ride takes about 30-40 minutes and costs around 50,000-70,000 Tanzanian shillings (around $20-30 USD) per person, depending on the type of boat and the time of day.

Take a Tour: Another option is to take a tour to Mnemba Atoll. There are several tour operators in Zanzibar that offer day trips to the atoll. These tours usually include transportation, snorkeling gear, and a guide.

Tumbatu Island

Located off the northwest coast of Zanzibar, Tumbatu Island is a hidden gem that is perfect for a day trip. This small island is known for its stunning beaches, crystal-clear waters, and vibrant coral reefs. Below is a guide to visiting Tumbatu Island as a day trip destination.

About Tumbatu Island

Tumbatu Island is a small island located about 10 kilometers off the northwest coast of Zanzibar. The island is about 6 kilometers long and 1 kilometer wide, and it's surrounded by stunning beaches and coral reefs. Tumbatu Island is a peaceful and serene destination that is perfect for relaxation and snorkeling.

Attractions and Activities

Snorkeling and Diving: The coral reefs surrounding Tumbatu Island are home to an incredible array of marine life, including sea turtles, rays, and colorful fish.

Beach Relaxation: The island has several stunning beaches that are perfect for relaxation. Enjoy the sun, sand, and sea, and take a break from the hustle and bustle of everyday life.

Swimming and Swimming with Dolphins: The waters surrounding Tumbatu Island are home to a pod of bottlenose dolphins. Take a swim with these incredible creatures and experience the thrill of a lifetime.

Fishing and Boat Trips: Tumbatu Island is a great destination for fishing and boat trips. Take a boat trip around the island and try your hand at fishing for some of the island's famous seafood.

How to Get to Tumbatu Island

Take a Ferry from Nungwi: The most common way to get to Tumbatu Island is by taking a ferry from Nungwi. The ferry ride takes about 30-40 minutes and costs around 5,000-10,000 Tanzanian shillings (around $2-5 USD) per person, depending on the type of ferry and the time of day.

Take a Private Boat: Another option is to take a private boat to Tumbatu Island. This option is more expensive than taking the ferry, but it offers more flexibility and comfort.

Join a Tour: Finally, you can also join a tour to Tumbatu Island. There are several tour operators in Zanzibar that offer day trips to the island. These tours usually include transportation, snorkeling gear, and a guide.

Chumbe Island

Located just off the coast of Zanzibar, Chumbe Island is a unique eco-resort that is perfect for a day trip. This small island is known for its stunning beaches, crystal-clear waters, and incredible marine life. Below is a guide to visiting Chumbe Island as a day trip destination.

About Chumbe Island

Chumbe Island is a small island located about 6 kilometers off the coast of Zanzibar. The island is about 1 kilometer long and 0.5 kilometers wide, and it's surrounded by stunning beaches and coral reefs. Chumbe Island is a protected area, and it's home to an incredible array of marine life, including sea turtles, rays, and colorful fish.

Attractions and Activities

Snorkeling and Diving: The coral reefs surrounding Chumbe Island are home to an incredible array of marine life. Take a snorkeling or diving trip to explore the reef and see some of the island's famous sea creatures.

Beach Relaxation: The island has several stunning beaches that are perfect for relaxation. Enjoy the sun, sand, and sea, and take a break from the hustle and bustle of everyday life.

Nature Walks: Chumbe Island is home to a range of unique flora and fauna. Take a nature walk around the island to explore the forest and see some of the island's unique wildlife.

Lighthouse Tour: The island's historic lighthouse is a must-visit attraction. Take a tour of the lighthouse to learn about its history and see some stunning views of the surrounding area.

How to Get to Chumbe Island

Take a Boat from Zanzibar Town: The most common way to get to Chumbe Island is by taking a boat from Zanzibar Town. The boat ride takes about 30-40 minutes and costs around 50,000-70,000 Tanzanian shillings (around $20-30 USD) per person, depending on the type of boat and the time of day.

Take a Private Boat: Another option is to take a private boat to Chumbe Island. This option is more expensive than taking the public boat, but it offers more flexibility and comfort.

Join a Tour: Finally, you can also join a tour to Chumbe Island. There are several tour operators in Zanzibar that offer day trips to the island. These tours usually include transportation, snorkeling gear, and a guide.

Chapter 13 • Sustainability and Responsible Travel

As a traveler to Zanzibar, you have the power to make a positive impact on the island and its people. Sustainability and responsible travel are essential for preserving the island's natural beauty, culture, and way of life. Below is a guide to help you travel responsibly and sustainably in Zanzibar.

Why Sustainability and Responsible Travel Matter in Zanzibar

Zanzibar is a fragile and vulnerable ecosystem that is heavily reliant on tourism. The island's coral reefs, forests, and wildlife are all under threat from climate change, overfishing, and pollution. By traveling responsibly and sustainably, you can help to reduce your impact on the environment and support local communities.

Tips for Sustainable and Responsible Travel in Zanzibar

Reduce Your Carbon Footprint: Consider offsetting your carbon emissions from flights and other transportation. You can also reduce your energy consumption by turning off lights and air conditioning when not in use.

Use Eco-Friendly Accommodations: Choose accommodations that are environmentally friendly and sustainable. Look for hotels and resorts that use solar power, have recycling programs, and implement sustainable waste management practices.

Respect Local Customs and Traditions: Zanzibar is a culturally rich and diverse island. Be respectful of local customs and traditions, and dress modestly when visiting mosques or other cultural sites.

Support Local Communities: Support local communities by buying local products, eating at local restaurants, and using local transportation. This will help to distribute tourism revenue more evenly and support local economic development.

Conserve Water and Energy: Conserve water and energy by taking shorter showers, turning off taps when not in use, and using energy-efficient appliances.

Reduce Waste and Litter: Reduce waste and litter by avoiding single-use plastics, recycling, and disposing of waste properly.

Respect Marine Life: Zanzibar's coral reefs and marine life are fragile and vulnerable. Respect marine life by not touching or standing on coral reefs, not feeding fish, and not littering.

Sustainable Tourism Initiatives in Zanzibar

Marine Conservation Projects: Support marine conservation projects that work to protect and conserve Zanzibar's coral reefs and marine life.

Community-Based Tourism Projects: Support community-based tourism projects that work to distribute tourism revenue more evenly and support local economic development.

Eco-Lodges and Sustainable Accommodations: Support eco-lodges and sustainable accommodations that use environmentally friendly and sustainable practices.

Sustainability and responsible travel are essential for preserving Zanzibar's natural beauty, culture, and way of life. By following these tips and guidelines, you can make a positive impact on the island and its people. Remember to respect local customs and traditions, support local communities, conserve water and energy, reduce waste and litter, and respect marine life. By traveling responsibly and sustainably, you can help to ensure that Zanzibar remains a beautiful and vibrant destination for generations to come.

Conclusion

As you come to the end of this Zanzibar travel guide, we hope that you're feeling inspired and excited to start planning your trip to this incredible island. From the stunning beaches and crystal-clear waters to the vibrant culture and rich history, Zanzibar has something for everyone.

Whether you're a seasoned traveler or embarking on your first adventure, Zanzibar is a destination that will leave you in awe. With its unique blend of African, Arab, and European influences, Zanzibar is a true melting pot of cultures.

As you explore the island, remember to take your time, be respectful of the local culture, and soak up the laid-back atmosphere. Try the local cuisine, visit the historic sites, and take a boat trip to one of the nearby islands.

Most importantly, remember that Zanzibar is a place of incredible beauty and diversity, but it's also a place with its own unique challenges and limitations. Be mindful of your impact on the environment and the local community, and take steps to reduce your footprint.

As you prepare to embark on your Zanzibar adventure, we hope that this guide has provided you with the inspiration, information, and insights you need to make the most of your trip. Whether you're looking for relaxation, adventure, or cultural immersion, Zanzibar has something for everyone.

So pack your bags, grab your sunscreen, and get ready for the adventure of a lifetime. Zanzibar, here you come!

Printed in Great Britain
by Amazon

57453309R00086